T0317602

Guide to CFO Success

Founded in 1807, John Wiley & Sons is the oldest independent publishing company in the United States. With offices in North America, Europe, Asia, and Australia, Wiley is globally committed to developing and marketing print and electronic products and services for our customers' professional and personal knowledge and understanding.

The Wiley Corporate F&A series provides information, tools, and insights to corporate professionals responsible for issues affecting the profitability of their company, from accounting and finance to internal controls and performance management.

Guide to CFO Success

*Leadership Strategies for
Corporate Financial Professionals*

SAMUEL DERGEL

WILEY

Copyright © 2014 by Samuel Dergel. All rights reserved.
Published by John Wiley & Sons, Inc., Hoboken, New Jersey.
Published simultaneously in Canada.

For general information on our other products and services or for technical support, please contact
our Customer Care Department within the United States at (800) 762-2974, outside the United
States at (317) 572-3993 or fax (317) 572-4002.

Wiley publishes in a variety of print and electronic formats and by print-on-demand. Some material
included with standard print versions of this book may not be included in e-books or in print-on-
demand. If this book refers to media such as a CD or DVD that is not included in the version you
purchased, you may download this material at http://booksupport.wiley.com. For more information
about Wiley products, visit www.wiley.com.

Library of Congress Cataloging-in-Publication Data :

Dergel, Samuel, 1969-
  Guide to CFO success : leadership strategies for corporate financial professionals / Samuel Dergel.
    pages cm. – (Wiley corporate F&A series)
  Includes index.
  ISBN 978-1-118-67499-4 (cloth); ISBN 978-1-118-87188-1 (ebk);
ISBN 978-1-118-87170-6 (ebk)
  1. Chief financial officers. 2. Career development. I. Title.
  HG4027.35.D47 2014
  658.15–dc23

                                                                                    2013044547

Printed in the United States of America
10 9 8 7 6 5 4 3 2 1

This book is dedicated to my grandparents, Clara and Hans Diestel.

Contents

Preface

WHO CARES ABOUT the **Chief Financial Officer?**

I do. And so should you.

Chief Financial Officers (CFOs) are cultural and business icons whose actions and decisions impact not only the companies they work for but nations. While the business media has been paying more attention to this Very Important Person over the past decade, general society has not given CFOs the attention they deserve. Our culture glamorizes other professions and business leaders without giving credit to the character that keeps businesses running and the cash flowing.

I do not expect this book to make a dent in the cultural status of the CFO. I do intend to inform CFOs themselves, as well as the people aiming to become CFOs, of their value and how they can take responsibility for their own success. I deal with CFOs every day. CFOs bring much more to the table than their technical expertise. There are books on leadership strategies for general business success. There are technical books aimed at CFOs. But I have not been able to find any leadership books for CFOs. I decided to write the first one.

I decided to write the first book dedicated to the success of the **Chief Financial Officer** because, based on my conversations with them as an executive recruiter and coach, I noticed that they need guidance. Senior finance executives are very talented individuals, yet I have found that many of them are either focused on their career or their employer at any given time. Only very successful CFOs understand that their personal success is based on the effort they put into their employer and their career and that focusing on both at the same time is not mutually exclusive.

The content for this book was not created in a vacuum. My ideas derive from the conversations and consulting I do as part of my practice as an executive recruiter and coach that has a very strong focus on the CFO and his or her team. Over the past years, with the encouragement of CFOs, I have blogged and written for and about **Chief Financial Officers** and the issues they face. Social media allowed me to get ideas across, but it did not allow me to share my comprehensive vision for what success means to CFOs, and how they can achieve it. Blogging, tweeting, and sharing information on LinkedIn allowed me to share some of my thoughts, but not enough. While social media is great for sharing individual thoughts, there is nothing like an "old media" book to share my thoughts on this subject in a comprehensive manner.

This book should be read by CFOs, future CFOs, and the people who work with these talented individuals.

CFOs will appreciate this book for the valuable ideas and strategies that will help them challenge themselves to improve in all aspects of their careers. If you are a **Chief Financial Officer**, parts of this book will make you feel as if I am speaking to you directly about the issues you are currently facing or have faced in your career. I'm sure there are leadership books that may be able to give you some great ideas, but there are no books out there written with an understanding of your unique role that bring you strategies for success from a perspective that you face every day.

Financial professionals who are on the path to becoming CFOs will find this book of significant value. Not only will it give you a real appreciation for what it looks and feels like at the top of **Finance**, but you will be able to prepare yourself for the reality of the challenges faced by the **Chief Financial Officer**. If you are hoping to make it to the top finance position in your career, you need to know that your success is not only about your technical skills. The information and strategies in this book will help you to understand the critical nontechnical skills that are also needed to prepare for a successful career as CFO.

If you interact with the CFO or the office of the **Chief Financial Officer**, reading this book will give you insights into the challenges faced by the CFO and an understanding of what they need to do to be successful. People without financial backgrounds who work with the CFO often say they find the CFO to be a challenge or an enigma. Not so. CFOs can be very easy to work with and for. Read this book and you will arm yourself with the understanding necessary to be successful in your relationship with corporate finance leaders.

Chapter 1 begins with a discussion about **Chief Financial Officers**, what makes them successful, and how they can balance life, work, and career on the road to success.

Part One of the book focuses on strategies for career success for the CFO. Chapter 2 discusses how a CFO can plan for career success. The third chapter reviews danger signs CFOs need to be aware of and avoid. Chapter 4 tackles the issue of moonlighting—focusing on projects outside of work. A conversation about the unemployed CFO is the basis for the fifth chapter, while Chapter 6 offers tips and strategies for CFOs about to start with a new company.

Part Two focuses on the other pillar of CFO success: being successful at the job. Chapter 7 deals with planning for success at your employer. Chapter 8 begins the discussion about the importance of relationships to the CFO, while Chapters 9 through 11 deal with specific strategies for relationship success with the people you work for and with. Chapter 12 concludes *Guide to CFO Success* with a conversation about how to build and develop the finance team that is crucial to the support of the CFO.

Acknowledgments

I N TODAY'S DAY and age, self-publishing an aggregation of one's thoughts is easier than ever. Yet as I complete my efforts to share my thoughts with you about what makes a CFO successful, I am very grateful to John Wiley & Sons for its support in making this book happen. Sheck Cho, my executive editor, has encouraged me and guided me from the idea that I should write a book to the proposal for this book to our agreement to the very challenging yet satisfying journey I faced in putting this book together. This is my first book, and I truly believe that if it were not for the efforts of Sheck and the team at Wiley, you would not be reading these words today.

Just as the CFO has a relationship map (see Chapter 8), I have my own relationship map. My success is due in large part to the relationships I have and continue to build and nurture. My key relationships are the people I work for, work with, and the people who support me.

The people I work for are my clients. These are the people who engage me to deliver the best executive search and coaching services possible. I enjoy every moment of working to meet their needs and their expectations. I am grateful for the trust they place in me. There is no better measure of success than being paid well for work that I love to do. My goal with this book is to help my executive search clients hire the very best financial professionals and guide my executive coaching clients to become the very best they can be.

The people I work with are my candidates. These people don't pay me in dollars, but they certainly pay me in appreciation. As I build relationships with these people, my investment of time in their careers pays off in spades. When the CFOs I deal with succeed, I succeed. I learn so much from these talented, motivated, and capable finance professionals. I could not have created this book without the countless hours I have spent with them on the phone and in their presence. You continue to inspire me.

I also work with my referrals. I am grateful to the accountants, lawyers, financial advisors, human resource consultants, and the countless others who think of me as the person who can solve challenges faced by their clients. These people open the trusted relationships they have with the people they work with and allow me to make them look good. These referrals are very important to me and thankfully are too numerous to mention by name.

The people who support me are the foundation for my being able to do what I do. Thankfully I have a few categories of these relationships.

You, my reader, support me by reading these pages. Unlike a blog or other social media channel, a book is not interactive. However, your feedback is important to me. Find me on LinkedIn and let me know what you like and don't like about this book. I would also love to hear about your stories of CFO success. I'm always looking for input on content focused on the CFO, so if you have an idea, let me know!

My CFO advisors were instrumental in creating relevant and valuable content to support the writing of this book. On a weekly basis over a period of three months in early 2013, my CFO advisors answered survey questions and shared comments about their experiences and perceptions of CFO reality. As you read this book, you will see a significant portion of their input. They took ideas I had surrounding the topic of CFO success and gave them life. I am sincerely grateful to them for their investment in my success and in yours.

I am especially indebted to three people who have supported and encouraged me to continue in my quest to create compelling content for and about the **Chief Financial Officer**. Chris Herbert, founder of Mi6 Agency, reached out to me two years ago and invited me to join CFO IXN (Intellectual Exchange Network), a select community of professionals who create content for and about the CFO. Chris has been a guide, mentor, motivator, and most importantly, a friend. Chris also introduced me to Sarah Shackley, a marketing director at SAP. I am very thankful to Sarah for her continued support of my creation of content aimed at the office of the **Chief Financial Officer**. Mitch Joel was the catalyst and motivator who got me started on the path that led to this book. His first book, *Six Pixels of Separation*, helped me develop an approach to my personal style of building relationships and gave me a framework upon which I was able to grow my business contacts and find different ways to continue to add value to them. I had the opportunity to sit down with Mitch in person and develop strategies and thoughts that were critical to the success of this book. Mitch, this book would never have been written if it weren't for you—thank you.

Stanton Chase International is the search firm that I work for. Yet, I consider them the team that supports me in the work that I do serving my clients. This firm is a collection of talented and experienced people who work together in more than 70 offices worldwide with the goal of helping our clients hire the very best. I am fortunate to have such a wonderful group helping me deliver outstanding talent surrounded by superb service. I would like to thank the firm and the people who work in it, specifically Paul Herrerias in San Francisco and Emerson Hughes in Montreal. Paul and Emerson support and challenge me in all my endeavors, and I continue to learn from them every day. Thank you both.

Last, but certainly not least, I would like to thank my friends and family. To my friends, and you know who you are, you have supported me in ways you aren't even aware of—thank you. To my family, you may find this hard to believe, but I don't know how to properly express the extent of my appreciation for everything you do for me. Each one of you means the world to me. To my wife, Reisha, I would like to publicly express that my achievements are only possible due to your continued love and support. I love you and I always will.

CFO Advisors

I N THE CREATION of *Guide to CFO Success*, I organized a group of senior finance executives to help me. Eighty-seven people signed up to be my advisors for this book. For a period of 14 consecutive weeks in early 2013, my advisors answered my questions and shared their personal experiences with me. These surveys were instrumental in providing me with real-world insight to the challenges faced by CFOs on their path to success. You will find their pearls of wisdom throughout this book.

I am truly grateful to all 87 of you for the investment you made. I hope you found it worth your time.

Thank you to the 59 people mentioned below who gave me permission to mention their names in this book. To the 28 who respectfully declined, don't worry. Your secret is safe with me.

Amy Brill Cooper	Art Stein	Bernard Baskin
Bill Milligan	Bob Shatanoff	Brenda I. Morris
Carrie E. McQueen	Christine Woolgar	Chuck Woods
Dale W. Boyles	Dan King	Dariusz Topczewski
David Cameron	David Schwartz	David Worachek
Dennis Ensing	Diane D. Lapp	Edward Schaffer
Eta Blitzer	Farid Chia Abdullah	Glenn Culpepper
Greg S. Levy	James Evanoff	Jeff Crystal
John P. Hamill	John Q. Farina	Jon Garfield
Jonathan Z. Kahan	Jonathon Levine	Joseph Patrick Duran
Kathleen A. Engel	Kenneth Tan	Kevin A. Paprzycki
Kevin Thompson	Larry N. Bloom	Leon Assayag
Linda Elphick	Lisa J. Kuruvilla	Mariano Rodriguez

Chief Financial Officer

T HERE ARE MANY ACCOUNTANTS and few Chief Financial Officers (CFOs). The accounting track is a popular starting point for many of today's CFOs, but accounting is certainly not the only road to the CFO role. Other popular starting points on the road to the CFO chair include investment banking and consulting.

Regardless of how they get there, CFOs' job descriptions depend a great deal on the companies they work for. A day in the life of a CFO at a large Fortune 500 company is most certainly different from that of a CFO at a small, entrepreneurial company. Yet they are both called the Chief Financial Officer.

In large companies, it is easy to define the difference between a CFO and a controller. At a smaller company, the most senior financial person may be called a CFO, but is he or she really the "Chief Financial Officer"?

The title "Chief Financial Officer" is well known in the business world. However, when you ask business people to define what a CFO is and what they do, they often find it difficult to describe.

WHAT IS A CHIEF FINANCIAL OFFICER?

In preparing to write this book, I felt it important to define what a CFO is—and is not.

Most of the books I have seen targeting the Chief Financial Officer are technical in nature and not leadership oriented. In these books, the definitions of the role of the CFO and the people who work for them read like a job description, defined by responsibilities and tasks performed by the CFO. I have found most of these definitions to be lacking. In my years of experience in executive search, I have seen that in reality, unlike the rigid descriptions provided in some texts, the tasks of Chief Financial Officers will vary by company size, industry, and growth stages of their businesses.

To gain a perspective on what a CFO is, I asked my 87 CFO advisors two open-ended questions on this topic. My CFO advisors were a key resource for me in the creation of this book. Coming from different backgrounds, industries, company sizes, and growth stages, they shared opinions, points of view, and personal experiences, all with the goal of assisting their peers.

Table 1.1 lists the most popular keywords my advisors used to respond to two questions.

My CFO advisors found that it was easier to define what a CFO is *not* than what a CFO is. In answer to the "not" question, most said CFOs were not accountants, bean counters, or number crunchers.

These words are essentially synonyms. My interpretation of what my CFO advisors were saying is, "Being CFO is not about being technical." I agree with them.

As I said previously, accounting is a popular way to begin the journey to becoming a Chief Financial Officer. While I come across many people who have the title CFO, not all of them are real CFOs. Why is that? Because the job they do is mostly technical in nature.

So what defines a real CFO? My CFO advisors say that Chief Financial Officers need to be strategists, leaders, and advisors.

TABLE 1.1 What Is and What Is Not a CFO?

What a CFO is not	What a CFO is
Accountant	Strategic
Bean counter	Leader
Number cruncher	Advisor

CFO as Strategist

My interest isn't sports. My interest is business. I follow business like many people follow sports. As an executive search consultant, I like to know the teams, the players, the strategies, and the score. While a sports fan can talk about strategy, it is the head coach of a sports team who makes decisions and plans based on a strategy. She or he works with all internal leaders to identify and execute strategy.

CFOs act as strategists when they make business decisions and prepare plans of action based on their companies' strategies. A strategic CFO is also a key contributor to and participant in the development and redefining of a company's strategy.

CFOs may have many responsibilities as they perform their functions, but if they are not acting and planning strategically for their businesses, they may not be real CFOs.

CFO as Leader

We can all think back through our careers and remember those people we worked with who were true leaders. During our formative career years, these people set examples for those of us who wanted to become leaders in our field.

Leaders set the pace, inspire, and act as an example for others.

CFOs are not only perceived as leaders for the people who work under their authority in finance but for other executives in the company, as well. The Chief Financial Officer may be a follower of the Chief Executive Officer who leads their company, but a successful CFO is looked at by the CEO as a fellow leader within the company.

CFO as Advisor

In my early days in recruitment, I helped a CFO hire a key person for his team. When it was time to make the person an offer, the CFO told me that one of the most important reasons this person should join his team was because he was able to offer the individual an opportunity to "add to the bag of tricks he will need as CFO."

CFOs have Solomon-like wisdom that comes from a combination of business smarts, experience gained from successes and failures, and an inherent understanding of the numerical logic that supports the making of sound business decisions combined with knowledge of profitable business operations.

The wisdom acquired by the CFO allows him or her to act as an advisor to the CEO and other executives in the business. CFOs who are considered advisors by other senior executives in the business and are sought out for their input and guidance in major business decisions are truly valued by the companies they work for.

 PERSONAL ATTRIBUTES OF A SUCCESSFUL CFO

You bought this book because you would like to know how you can become a (more) successful CFO. We defined what a CFO is not and what a CFO is. Successful CFOs also demonstrate the following personal attributes:

- A positive, can-do attitude
- Respect for the people they work with
- Egos that are firmly in check
- Emphasis on maintaining excellent relationships
- A deep desire to make a difference
- The desire to have fun

Positivity

A Chief Financial Officer faces challenges every day. Having a positive, can-do attitude gives the CFO the strength to deal with these challenges while being a positive role model for the people the CFO works for and with.

One CFO recently told me that people look to him internally to stay positive and move forward. As the CFO is the one with the firmest grasp of an organization's financial situation, people look to the CFO for an indication of how things are going. When the CFO is positive about the current situation and outlook, others inside and outside the business gain comfort from that attitude.

Respect

When CFOs are respected, they are able to accomplish great things because people listen to them and seriously consider their point of view. The ability to convince others is the hallmark of a great CFO. Before others will listen to you, they must respect you. To gain the respect of others, you need to give respect to others.

CFOs who give respect to all the people they come across every day—not just those with whom they work directly—gain the respect of these same people.

Irv Lichtenwald, currently CEO at Medsphere Systems Corporation, was a successful Chief Financial Officer earlier in his career. Lichtenwald believes respect is a key attribute for a CFO's success. Showing respect and acknowledging all the people you come in contact with, whether they are CEOs or receptionists, fellow CFOs or clerical staff, investment bankers or bank tellers, executives within your business or maintenance people, earns the respect of others. Following this advice has been a key attribute to his career success, Lichtenwald said.

Ego

As CFO, keeping your ego in check allows you to continue to be successful. It is easy for a successful CFO with a track record of making a significant difference for the companies for which he has worked to allow himself to begin believing all the positive reviews.

Realizing that there is always room to improve and become a better CFO will ensure you keep on improving and raising the bar.

One of my CFO advisors shared this pearl of wisdom. "As you climb the corporate ladder, fewer and fewer people give you honest feedback and this creates a leadership blindside." Understand that not all the feedback you receive is complete. Realize that there is always room to learn, improve, and grow.

CFOs who are aware of their egos and keep them in check are successful CFOs.

Relationships

A Chief Financial Officer cannot work alone. CFOs need to interact with other people to do their jobs. Those who place importance on maintaining and nurturing excellent relationships will increase their odds of success.

A large part of this book addresses CFO relationships (Chapters 8 through 12). In these chapters you will learn more about how you can improve your relationships with the various people with whom you must interact.

Bill Koefoed, previously CFO at Skype, believes that having strong relationships allows the CFO to accomplish and succeed. "Relationships," says Bill, "are obviously very important to the success of a CFO."

Making a Difference

Successful CFOs are driven people. What motivates a successful CFO?

CFOs want to accomplish. CFOs have a deep desire to make a difference. They want to succeed. They want to do something significant with their careers. They want to contribute and be key players in making substantial things happen for the organizations they work for, the people who work for the business as well as the owners.

Irv Lichtenwald told me that he has enjoyed making a difference. He said that "when you believe in the cause of whatever firm you are with, and you believe there is real value to what you are doing, then it makes it easier for a CFO to go ahead and be successful."

Have Fun

When CFOs are having fun at work, they are at the top of their game. When they get bored and don't enjoy the game anymore, they cannot provide the best they have to offer to their employer.

When a CFO starts a new position with a new company, it is easy to have fun. As time goes on, a CFO is usually having less fun as he or she becomes more involved with the company and becomes a magnet for problems that need solving that can't be addressed anywhere else in the company.

Lichtenwald said he believes that having fun is a key to success for a CFO. "If you're having fun, it makes it easier for you to be successful."

To continue having fun, CFOs need to know what they enjoy doing as well as what they don't. Being responsible for something doesn't mean you have to do it yourself; it just means you have to ensure it gets done. Structuring your finance team so as to allow you to handle those things you enjoy lets you ensure you deliver what you've committed to while still having fun. We discuss this more in Chapter 12, Building and Developing Your Finance Team.

 ## SKILLS REQUIRED FOR CFO SUCCESS

While personal attributes are important to the success of a CFO, she or he also needs strong skills.

Current CFO at Puppet Labs, Inc., Bill Koefoed (CFO of Skype at time of interview), said there are three things needed to succeed as a CFO: finance skills, strategic thinking, and the ability to communicate. His perspective is represented in Figure 1.1.

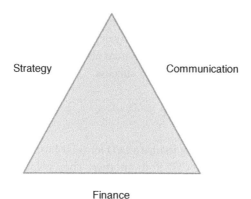

FIGURE 1.1 Skills Required for CFO Success

Finance Skills

"First, you obviously need to have really good finance skills, but there are a lot of people who have those," Koefoed said. Strong finance skills are a key part of the foundation to becoming a CFO. Over the years, finance professionals need to continue adding to their bags of tricks. However, without investing time and energy in building these key skills, a finance professional cannot become a good CFO. As Koefoed says, strong skills in finance are necessary, but they do not differentiate you from others.

Strategic Thinker

The second skill a good CFO needs is to be a strategic thinker, Koefoed says. "CFOs who come from banking or consulting backgrounds have generally been trained well in this area," he noted. The ability to think strategically is one area that can help CFOs differentiate themselves. Generally, CFOs who come from an investment banking or consulting background have training and experience that gives them an edge in this area over those with accounting backgrounds. For those with an accounting background, gaining hands-on strategic experience can help set them apart from the pure finance-trained CFOs.

Communication Skills

Koefoed told me that "CFOs need good communication skills. You need to be a really good salesman, whether it's selling your ideas or selling the company to investors. You need to be able to sell your ideas." Unless CFOs are trained to improve their communication skills, they are working with their natural, unpolished communication talents. In my experience, CFOs who can effectively communicate their positions and convince others of their points of view truly have an advantage on their road to success.

CFOs ARE DIFFERENT

Some people who are looking to hire a CFO for their business believe that there is little to differentiate one CFO from another. They want to hire a "numbers person" who can help their business be "more successful."

Some CFOs who are looking for their next career opportunity also believe there is little difference between CFOs. CFOs who find themselves between opportunities and looking for their next role often have an "I can do anything" attitude. This attitude can lead them to accept job offers that they will regret, because the role they were hired for will not take advantage of the value they can bring to the table.

The reality is that CFOs are different—they have different skills, knowledge, and experience. The companies that hire CFOs need to hire the best CFOs for their businesses. Because businesses are different, the CFOs they hire need to be different, as well.

What Kind of CFO Is Right for My Company?

Before a company can choose the right CFO for its needs, it needs to understand what its needs are. The type of CFO a particular company needs is based on where it is on the growth spectrum. Companies fall into the following phases:

- **Start-up.** This company is in the organization stage of putting its business together. The founders focus on building their business based on an idea built around a need a potential customer might have. It might be pre-revenue or in the early stages of revenue, and the founders are looking to find the right formula to grow this business.
- **Growth.** Companies in growth mode are going through rapid change and are exciting companies to work for. Their growth can be organic, which comes from natural revenue increases based on increased customer demand, or it can derive from acquisition of another business or from a mixture of organic and acquisition growth.
- **Status quo.** Many companies maintain their business over a period of time. They do what they do well enough to stay in business but are not

innovating and focusing on growing the business, nor are they failing and declining. Companies in this category can have varying degrees of profitability, but many CFOs may not find them an exciting place to work.

▪ **Restructure.** When owners (or creditors) choose to make radical changes to a company to ensure survival of the company or at least that the company can pay what it owes, the company is in the restructuring phase. This phase can be very stressful on the people who are involved with the company. Decisions are made in this situation that can be quick and painful. Many times a company ends up in this situation because of mismanagement, but economic headwinds can be a key reason, as well.

Companies in each of these phases require their own types of CFO. CFOs with experience in one type of company are less likely to be successful with another type of company.

My CFO advisors were asked the following question: "What are the top three strengths needed by CFOs working for companies in these various phases?" Here is a summary of the most common answers given by my advisors.

Start-Up

▪ Manage cash.
▪ Attract and maintain investors.
▪ Be a generalist.

Growth

▪ Manage cash.
▪ Attract and maintain investors and bankers.
▪ Be a strategist.

Status Quo

▪ Manage cash and costs.
▪ Focus on processes for efficiencies.
▪ Master communication skills.

Restructure

▪ Manage cash and costs.
▪ Master communication skills.
▪ Attract and maintain investors and bankers.

When Companies Hire Their CFO

If CFOs are different from one another, and companies are different, too, what should a company be looking for when hiring a CFO?

Companies need to be aware that hiring the wrong CFO can have a very negative impact on the company. Hiring the wrong CFO can lead to increased cost of capital, the inability to access capital when needed, not meeting corporate financial objectives, and losing key talent critical to the company.

Before a company hires its next (or first) CFO, it needs to ensure it understands what it needs from its CFO. Understanding the stage your business is in and what your business needs from your finance leader is critical. Companies must prioritize the importance of their needs, as well.

Companies also need to realize that they may not be able to hire the person who has everything they feel they need. For one, it may not be possible to find someone who has the ability to do everything you need. And even if you were able to find someone who can do everything himself, there may not be enough time for him to deliver on this.

The most effective CFO is the one who is able to ensure delivery in all areas needed by the company. CFOs don't need to be experts in everything; they just need to be experts in ensuring delivery for all the company needs.

When CFOs Get Hired

CFOs need to take the time to really understand the needs of the company they are interviewing with. Not only do CFOs need to present themselves as the best solution based on what the company needs (as the company explains it), they also need to put on their consulting hats and ask probing questions to identify what it is that the company they are speaking with really needs. Only once the CFO candidate understands the company's real needs can she assess whether she is the best CFO to meet that company's needs, and sell herself accordingly. This is the clarity a CFO needs so that once she gets hired, she can meet and exceed the expectations of the people she will be working for.

Too many CFOs sell themselves for a role saying that they can do the job. Successful CFOs ensure that when they are hired for a role, they are the best fit for their new employer's needs.

CFOs should only want to be hired for a role that will match their knowledge, skills, and abilities as well as their career plans. Career planning for the CFO is further discussed in Chapter 2.

WORK–LIFE BALANCE

One of the biggest challenges faced by senior finance professionals is one of balance. Work–life balance continues to be a challenge in corporate America today. In the era before mobile phones, only medical professionals, plumbers, and electricians had beepers and needed to be available at all times to respond to an emergency.

In the not-too-distant past, there was a border between a person's personal life and work life. Today, this border is blurred. The proliferation of mobile devices contributes to an "always-on" lifestyle, where professionals are always on call.

Finance professionals are known to send and receive work-related messages on their smartphones or tablets at all hours of the day and evening, and sometimes in the middle of the night. Being connected and available is a requirement in today's business environment. Compliance-related deadlines are shorter and stricter. More work must be done in less time. This requires finance professionals to work from mobile devices outside of work hours.

Weekends and vacations are no longer sacred personal time in corporate America, especially for corporate finance professionals. Finance people tell me that they are expected to be always available. Some CFOs have told me that when they want a real break, they travel to an area without cell phone coverage, even as such areas are more and more difficult to find.

Always-on does have advantages. It does give professionals the flexibility to take time for the personal and important nonwork moments in their life, while ensuring that the work gets done and that decisions are made. Being able to attend a child's soccer game during work hours or attend a medical appointment with a loved one while being available and connected to your work colleagues does offer flexibility. Employees appreciate not being tied to their desks while still being able to make a difference at work.

The challenge is and continues to be, "How do I balance it all?"

CFOs are leaders for their finance team and for the company. How they act sets the standard for how others are expected to act. When a Chief Financial Officer stays late at the office on most nights, staff understand that they are expected to do the same. When a CFO sends emails at 2 A.M. expecting an answer by 9 A.M., the message that is being sent is not only the request in the email.

However, when a CFO attends his child's soccer game and makes himself available to his employees and peers, or when a CFO takes a real vacation, he or she sets an example, as well.

Being aware that work–life balance is necessary and important, both for you as CFO, and your team, is of the utmost importance.

THE OTHER IMPORTANT THING TO BALANCE

When people talk about work–life balance, the work portion is generally thought of as the work they do for their employer.

When I think of work, I see it as two distinct yet inextricably related components: career and employment.

For senior finance professionals to become and continue to stay successful, they must focus on both their careers *and* their employment. I have never seen a successful CFO who is only successful in one or the other; they must be successful at both.

If you remember nothing else from reading this book, remember this: *You can be a successful CFO only if you focus on both your career and your employer.*

CFOs who focus solely on delivering the maximum value to their employers and do not focus on continuing to develop their careers will not continue to be successful CFOs. Chief Financial Officers cannot be successful if they focus on advancing their careers while not giving the best of themselves to their employers and the task at hand.

Most CFOs I speak with agree that they need to focus on their careers and their employers. The challenge many of them face is that they are very focused on giving their all to their employers.

It is my experience that CFOs and corporate finance professionals on the path to CFO are very hard workers. This experience led me to ask my CFO advisors the following question: "How much effort do you feel you put into your CFO role?" Their answers are graphically represented in Figure 1.2.

More than three-quarters of my CFO advisors told me that they put at least 110 percent effort into their CFO roles. When looking at this response, it seems that CFOs face an obvious challenge. How can they possibly find the time to focus on their careers when most say they are putting more than 110 percent effort into their responsibilities at their employers?

The answer is that CFOs and corporate finance professionals have no choice but to ensure they focus on their careers, even when they are giving all of their effort to their employers.

How is this possible? A popular saying is that if you want something done, give it to a busy person.

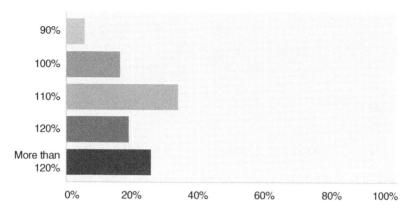

FIGURE 1.2   How Much Effort Do You Feel You Put into Your CFO Role?

Busy people have the ability to get a lot of things done. Busy people who understand their priorities are able to manage them well. There are many successful executives who make their personal lives a priority in addition to their work lives. Being successful at work does not preclude having a successful personal life. It is a question of balancing priorities.

Just as work and life can be balanced, career and employment can be balanced, as well. It is a matter of understanding that career needs to be a priority in addition to focusing on employment.

CFO success requires a healthy balance between a focus on career and employer. That is why this book is divided in two parts, Successful Career Strategies for the CFO (Chapters 2 through 6) and Successful Employment Strategies for the CFO (Chapters 7 through 12). I have provided strategies for success in these two areas because CFOs need to focus on both to be successful.

 CAREER VERSUS EMPLOYER: A QUESTION OF ETHICS?

Stories of corrupt and crooked CFOs and other corporate finance professionals receive a lot of attention. It is hard for such stories not to attract attention.

Financial misbehavior and unethical finance people get such attention because of the high level of trust society places in finance professionals, and because such stories are few and far between.

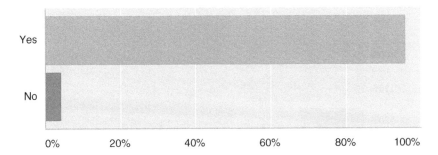

FIGURE 1.3 Is It Ethical to Look Out for Your Career When You Are Currently Employed?

There are millions of people working in finance roles at companies and organizations, yet there are only handfuls of stories of corruption and monkey business. There is a reason that there is a huge gap between the millions of honest financial professionals and the handful of those who are not honest.

Finance people consider themselves to be very ethical. I can think of many stories told to me in confidence by senior finance professionals about the ethical dilemmas they faced in their career. This led me to ask my CFO advisors: "Is it ethical to look out for your career when currently employed?" See Figure 1.3 for their answer.

I have to say that I was pleasantly surprised with this response. My experience has told me that not enough finance professionals give proper attention to their careers when they are employed. I've always wanted to know why most CFOs did not give enough attention to their careers.

I knew that the CFOs of today and tomorrow wanted to give attention to their careers, but for some reason did not. The answer to this question tells me that it is not their ethics getting in the way of focusing on their careers.

What Is Getting in the Way?

So what is getting in the way of finance professionals focusing on their careers?

There are many reasons why CFOs do not focus on their careers as much as they should. Time, or the lack of it, is always a good excuse. Many CFOs have told me that they have not needed to focus on their careers to be successful—they just had to work hard, and the fruits of promotions and new opportunities fell into their laps.

Focusing on work alone as a means to success for finance professionals can only work in the beginning of their careers. Once they reach the point in their careers where they need to focus on the strategic, advisory, and leadership aspects of being a senior finance professional, working hard alone is not enough.

My CFO advisors provided me with some excellent comments on the challenges of focusing on their careers. Here are some examples.

- I am completely focused on the success and well-being of my company, but it's important to be aware of the marketplace and the opportunities available to find a position that may be even a better match for my skills.
- It is ethical to look out for your career when employed. The problem for me is lack of time.
- You should always be focusing on your career. You never know when you may be looking again for a new job.
- As I look out for myself, I am still giving 110 percent to my employer.
- Looking out for your career takes many forms, and most are appropriate and beneficial to your current employer: ongoing education, networking with industry and technical peers, maintaining ethical standards of lines you will not cross, and being open and educational when communicating those standards to other executives.
- You have to always look out for your career. At the same time, when putting in 120 percent, it is very difficult to do so. I feel that this contributes to the time between positions.

 ## FOCUSING ON YOUR CAREER HELPS YOUR EMPLOYER

It is my premise that looking out for your career while employed not only helps your career, but your employer, as well.

How can that be?

Visibility

When you take steps to take care of your career while employed, you are making yourself visible. Your employer gains when you are visible in your community and industry. You are one of the top executives of the company. Representing your company while being visible makes your company look good.

Skills

Learning new things that grow your knowledge, enhance your skills, and improve your abilities certainly adds value to you. They also add value to your employer. As the key stakeholder in getting the best out of you, your employer has most to gain when you increase your knowledge, skills, and abilities. You gain personally because these become part of you, and will continue with you in the future when you work for another company.

Think about the following. You were hired by your current employer because of the knowledge, skills, and abilities you have brought with you. Almost all of this was learned in a formal or informal setting at the previous employers you've had in your life.

Becoming a better CFO or corporate finance professional adds value to you and your employer. If your employer fears that improving yourself would be detrimental to its interests, maybe you shouldn't be working there.

 CONCLUSION

- We defined what a CFO is.
- We defined five personal attributes of a successful CFO.
- We identified three skills required for CFO success.
- We identified that individual CFOs are different, and that companies have different needs for CFOs.
- We discussed the importance of CFOs balancing all aspects of their lives, and that work should be defined as commitment to both employer and career.
- We discussed that when CFOs are loyal to their employers, this can work to their disadvantage.
- We saw that to be successful, CFOs need to focus on career strategies as well as employment strategies. CFOs are able to truly succeed by focusing on both at the same time. At minimum, if employed, CFOs who ignore their

career do so to their detriment, and it limits them from becoming or continuing to be successful CFOs.

In the coming chapters, *Guide to CFO Success* provides the reader with strategies to get the best out of their career and their employer. Part One speaks to Employment Strategies for CFO Success, while Part Two identifies how current or future CFOs can set themselves up for continued success at their employer.

PART ONE

Successful Career Strategies for the CFO

THE PREMISE OF THIS BOOK is that CFO success requires two elements:

1. Success in your career (long term)
2. Success with your current employer (limited term)

My premise about CFO success is simple, yet very hard to accomplish on an ongoing basis.

You cannot have career success without employment success, and you cannot have employment success without career success. Becoming a better CFO benefits your employer and your career.

Many of the senior corporate financial professionals I speak with do not give their careers enough thought while they are successful and busy in their current employment. Successful financial professionals as a whole are generally very hard workers, and give 110 percent plus to the companies they work for. Too many of these finance professionals forget about nurturing their careers. They think that the best they can do for their careers is to hunker down and focus on delivering at their current employers, and being the best CFO or senior financial professional they can be. They believe that their reputation will stand up for them and help them move along in their career if (when) they are out of work.

In my experiences speaking with CFOs in transition (i.e., without a current job and looking for their next one), I have found that most did not prepare enough for the time when they would be in transition. The people most surprised by the idea that they had to focus on their careers are the individuals who have never had to search for a job before.

Finance people are in demand—at a junior level. A career pyramid exists for finance professionals. There are many financial analyst positions available but few CFO positions. The career sweet spot for a financial professional is the 5- to 10-, maybe 12-year window. This is where they are trained and experienced enough to be able to deliver at a high level of analysis work but are not overly expensive to their employers.

The further you want to move up the corporate ladder, the fewer opportunities will present themselves to you. To be able to continue to move up the corporate ladder and achieve and grow, you need to realize that there are more people competing for fewer positions.

Part One of this book provides CFOs of today and tomorrow with strategies for career success. These strategies are specifically targeted to these corporate financial professionals. By following these steps, you will set in motion the positive forces that will properly place you on the path to CFO success.

CHAPTER TWO

Planning for Career Success

CHIEF FINANCIAL OFFICER CAREER success requires planning. CFOs will agree that for a business to be successful, it needs a well-thought-out and vetted business plan. However, when planning their own business (otherwise known as their *career*), my experience has shown that few CFOs have a formal business plan of their own.

To gain an understanding of whether CFOs have personal career plans, I asked my CFO advisors whether they had a career plan, and if they did, whether it was formal or informal (see Figure 2.1). While 74 percent of my CFOs said they had a career plan, only 8 percent of them had a formal plan while over 25 percent had no career plan at all.

There are many individual CFOs who are very successful yet have never had a career plan, formal or informal. Why should a current or future CFO develop one?

Many CFOs have been successful not only because they are talented but because they were in the right place at the right time in their careers. This provided them with opportunity and choice, which they were able to make the best of.

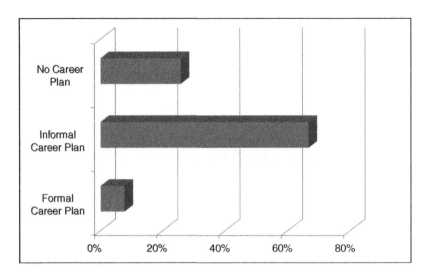

FIGURE 2.1　Career Plan

Perhaps that's called luck. When things go well, people feel that they are in control and can make a difference. When things are not going so well, people may not feel as in control. Do CFOs feel in control of their careers?

More than three-quarters of my CFO respondents felt that they have control over their careers (Figure 2.2). As one of my CFOs told me, "You create your own destiny."

I surveyed my CFO advisors in the beginning of 2013. If this question had been asked in 2007 or in 2009, the response might have been different. Current economic circumstances will always have an impact on whether senior financial executives feel in control of their careers.

Here are some interesting comments made by my CFO advisors on the topic of control over their careers. These comments reflect the diversity of responses on career control for CFOs.

> Even though I am currently seeking a new CFO opportunity, I believe that I have control over where my career goes next. I wish that I had prepared a more formal career plan and worked with a coach earlier in my career.
> If I don't control my career, who does?
> I have a view of where my career should go, but it largely depends on the opportunities presented.

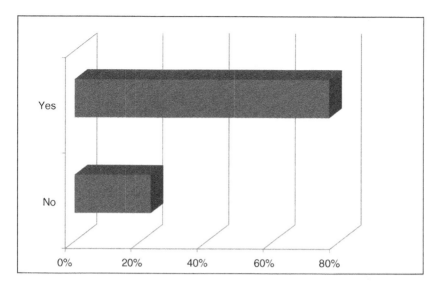

FIGURE 2.2 Do You Feel You Have Control over Your Career?

I do not have control due to being in my early 60s. When I was in my 40s, I controlled my career.

I have previously left, voluntarily, a very attractive CFO position because the environment did not correspond to my core values. I am ultimately responsible to make sure I seek career opportunities that fit with my goals and beliefs.

The following discussion provides some strategies to follow that will allow you to prepare a plan that will help guide your career.

PLAYING TO YOUR STRENGTHS

Successful CFOs always play to their strengths. They know their strengths and focus on improving them. CFOs use their strengths to the advantage of the company they work for, the people that work for them, and ultimately, themselves.

Successful CFOs also realize that they need to deliver beyond their strengths. Solid CFOs know that they need to have a supporting cast that will ensure that they can focus on their strengths, and still deliver in areas where they are not strong.

Before building on your strengths, you need to know what they are. Have you ever had them identified objectively?

Technical Strengths

Your strengths include your technical skills as well as your personal skills. As mentioned, having strong technical skills is not enough to make you a successful CFO. It is a start, though.

It is important to identify your technical skills, as they are one way that you can stand out. Remember, technical skills are usually the skills that you enjoy doing most, and you are known for these by others.

My CFO advisors were asked to share their top-three technical strengths. The most popular technical strengths among them were:

1. Planning and analysis
2. Accounting and reporting
3. Strategy

What are your top-three technical strengths?

1. _____
2. _____
3. _____

Personal Strengths

For technically trained finance professionals, it can be relatively easy to identify their technical skills. Where it can become difficult for finance professionals to be objective is when they are asked to identify their personal strengths.

There are a number of tools that can help identify personal strengths. One effective yet inexpensive tool that I use in my coaching is the Clifton Strengths-Finder assessment. The tool, which is available with the book, *Strengths-Based Leadership*, is an online test that can provide you with insights that you can use to become even stronger.

Of my CFO advisors, 64 percent have used an objective assessment tool to identify their personal strengths. I highly recommend that any current or future CFOs understand objectively what their personal strengths are, as it gives them an opportunity to capitalize on them.

Not only do I believe this to be true, but almost all of the respondents who took a formal assessment agreed that it was useful to them personally. One of my CFOs said that "it's always helpful to get feedback on your strengths and weaknesses in a manner that does not get filtered by being 'what you want to hear' versus 'what you need to hear.'"

Like I did for technical strengths, I also asked my CFO advisors what they believed to be their top-three personal strengths. The three most popular answers they gave me are:

1. Communication
2. Leadership
3. Ethics

What are your top-three personal strengths?

1. _____
2. _____
3. _____

PERSONAL BRAND

You are a CFO. You say you are. Your business card says you are. Your employer calls you its Chief Financial Officer. The teams of people you work with refer to you as the CFO. So, you must be a CFO.

Answer this: What kind of CFO are you? What is your brand? How do others perceive you? There are no easy answers to these questions.

Do you need to answer these questions? Yes. Are they relevant? Yes. Does it matter what kind of CFO you are? Absolutely.

What Is a Personal Brand?

To learn more about personal branding, I spoke with Karen Wensley, author of *The Power of Personal Branding for Career Success*. The book discusses personal branding in detail, and provides examples and work tools that can help you identify and develop your own personal brand.

Wensley says that "every financial professional already has a brand. It might not be the brand that they want, and it might not be the brand they

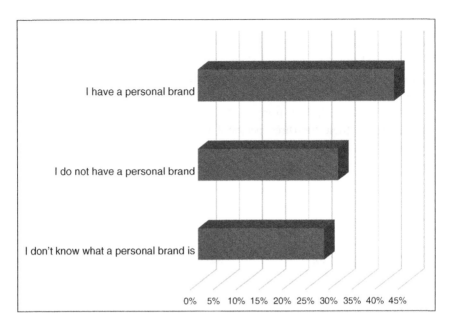

FIGURE 2.3 Personal Brand: Do CFOs Have One?

think they have. People make decisions about you based on what they know about you." She also says that "if you're not actively thinking about what that brand is, you are missing opportunities. You have a brand. You might as well manage it."

Considering the importance of personal branding for the career of a senior finance professional, I asked my CFO advisory group if they had a personal brand (Figure 2.3). To my delight, 42 percent of my respondents said they have a personal brand, while the remainder either did not have one or did not know what a personal brand is.

Some of the personal brands of my CFO advisors include:

- Strategic and operational CFO focused on value creation.
- Financial leadership for high-tech hardware companies.
- I bring structure to chaos.
- The voice of reason.
- Creative financial ideation put into practice.

Your Personal Brand and Your Employer

You want to work for an employer that will not only appreciate you, but will want to get the best out of you, as well. Any employer that wants to hide you behind the coattails of the CEO or behind a desk will not help you develop your personal brand.

You may be happy or satisfied being a behind-the-scenes finance executive. This is fine and certainly acceptable as it is your choice. I would caution you that taking this path will not provide you with career opportunities that will find you.

Wensley believes that some people shy away from thinking about their personal brand because "they think it is selfish. As a matter of fact, it is not selfish at all. Assuming that you're in the workplace because you want to help your colleagues and your community, thinking strongly about 'how am I going to be most helpful to all those entities' is really the same thing as thinking about 'what is my brand?'"

How to Brand Yourself

Branding requires that you know what you are good at (and like to do), and that others know what you are good at (and like to do).

How do you know what you are good at?

- You identify your technical skills.
- You identify and assess your personal skills.
- You get feedback, both formal and informal, from people who know you and work with you professionally, on what they believe you are good at.

How do you get others to know about you?

- Networking.
- Visibility on social media.
- Representing your employer externally or your group internally.

What is your personal brand?

 NETWORKING

Career opportunities (internal and external) can only find you when you are visible. The first step to standing out in a crowd is standing up. It requires action on your part. Sitting at your desk and at the wheel of your car do not allow other people to know you.

Too many people start reaching out to their network when they are actively looking for their next career opportunity. A network will work for you when you need it only if you have invested in it first.

Nearly 60 percent of my CFO advisors said that networking was the one thing they should be doing more of to have a greater impact on their career. When my CFOs were asked to compare how effective they felt they were in networking compared to how effective they would like to be at networking, I received these results (Figure 2.4).

CFOs agree that networking is important, yet they feel that they need to do more networking and to do it more effectively. So what is their reason for not networking? Over two-thirds of my group said that they are just too busy. Another interesting reason given was that CFOs do not want to be sold to.

I asked my CFO advisors to provide me with one example of how networking had a direct impact on their career. This is what they had to say.

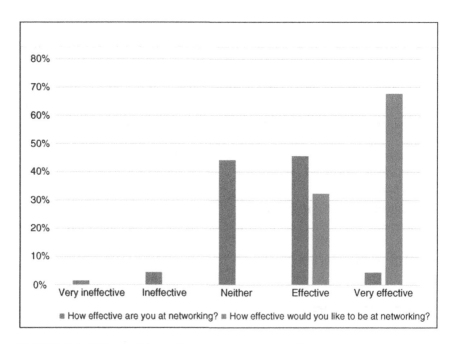

FIGURE 2.4 Effective Networking

Networking is a fundamental part of being a CFO and by networking throughout my career I was ready to step into the CFO job for a large corporation.

Network contacts have provided a sounding board on strategy and profitable ideas.

Can't think of one specifically, probably since I'm not that good at it!

I chair an industry CFO taskforce. This has had a direct impact on my profile and credibility.

All eight of my senior/CFO or board/advisory roles have come via referral, recommendation, or networking.

There is a belief (which is incorrect) that all someone needs to do is to have a profile on LinkedIn and add people to your LinkedIn network. There is certainly a value to social media, but social media is a tool that assists with networking effectively. It does not replace networking; it supports it.

Networking Is a Verb

Having a network is not enough. You build a network by actively networking. Your network has to be valuable to you. Your network is a career investment. The only way to have a return on investment is to make the investment in the first place.

How Do You Create a Valuable Network?

To build the value of your network, you need to build it before expecting a return. Too many individuals network with the purpose of accomplishing an immediate goal. That's not networking; that's selling.

There is nothing wrong with selling. The challenge for finance professionals is that too many of them get uncomfortable when someone is trying to sell to them, but when they need something from someone they have no problem calling people and asking for something (i.e., "I'm looking for a job—can you find something for me?").

The successful networkers I know are able to ask for something from their network. In most cases, they have given in advance (paid it forward) to their network before asking for anything in return. They know that the best way to receive is to give. Those that win in networking give first, give generously, and give often.

Networkers who give to others are known by others to be generous, and will receive what they need from others. Networking reputation follows and pays off.

Get Uncomfortable

Too many CFOs network with other CFOs. They do so because it is more comfortable to talk to other CFOs. Is this the most valuable way to spend precious time dedicated to networking? Rather than dedicate time to meeting other finance executives, speak to potential referral sources, such as lawyers, accountants, and bankers.

Another great place to network is within your industry. Competitors, suppliers, and customers can provide you with business insights that can be very valuable to you and your employer. These conversations may even lead to business or career opportunities.

The value you will get from networking with people you don't know yet is higher than the value of networking with people you've known for years who are in the same situation as you are.

Size Does Not Matter

Networking should be focused and targeted. Networking should not take a shotgun approach. The size of your network doesn't matter—it is the quality of your network that counts. The quality of your network can be measured by whether and how quickly people in your network will return your call when you reach out to them.

What follows is a list of networking strategies that will allow you to build and maintain a quality network.

Places to Network in Person

- Conferences
- Cocktails
- Scheduled meetings
- Networking groups
- Personal relationships (hobbies, interests, activities)

How to Network

- First rule: Go to the event.
- Set goals before the meeting.

- Add value before requesting value.
- Become a known resource to your network.
- Continuously learn how to improve your networking.

 ## SOCIAL MEDIA FOR THE CFO

Social media is popular with CFOs. The most popular tool for senior finance professionals is LinkedIn, according to a survey of my CFO advisors (Figure 2.5). All of the CFOs in my advisory group use LinkedIn, with 95 percent of them using it at least once a week.

Before surveying my CFOs, I had thought that LinkedIn usage was lower. My weekly blog, *CFO Moves*, is the most comprehensive report on CFO movements across the United States. Each person mentioned in my *CFO Moves* blog has a hyperlink to their LinkedIn profile if they have one. Not every CFO

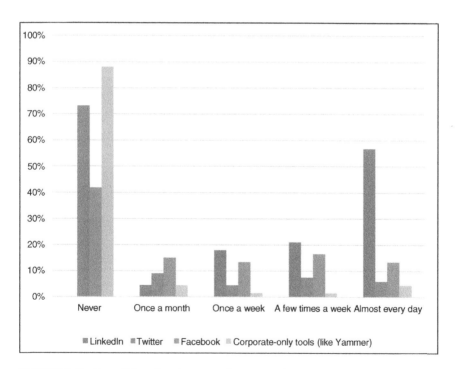

FIGURE 2.5   How Often Do You Use These Social Media Tools?

who gets a new job has a LinkedIn profile, but considering the popularity of LinkedIn for professionals in today's day and age, a CFO who is not on LinkedIn is almost certainly missing opportunities.

My CFO advisors use other well-known social media tools, but none are as popular with them as LinkedIn. I was not surprised that Twitter was not a popular tool (only 27 percent of the group said they used it at all), but I was surprised that 42 percent of my group said that they never use Facebook. Corporate-only networking tools like Yammer have a small following, but I believe that this will grow in use in the coming years, as internal networking in larger organizations is very important to career success inside these businesses.

Social media may be popular for CFOs, but is time spent on social media effective for CFOs? My CFOs agree by an overwhelming majority (85 percent) that time spent on LinkedIn is either effective or very effective. (See Figure 2.6.)

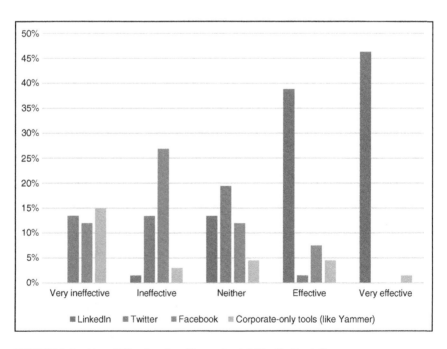

FIGURE 2.6　How Effective Are These Social Media Tools?

Here is what my CFO advisors had to say about the value of social media to them.

> I believe that social media has an impact on our personal lives and can be used effectively to increase networking opportunities. It cannot be a replacement for face-to-face networking and should only be used as one tool in your networking toolbox.
> Social media is a widely held method of networking, conducting business, and socializing. It isn't going away, so you had better learn how to extract value from it or you'll be left behind!
> Keeps me abreast of things but can also be another large time sink if I'm not cautious and focused.
> You get out of it what you put into it. It's like practicing the piano. The more you do it, the more benefit you get.
> I use Facebook as a personal tool to stay in touch with friends and family. I use LinkedIn as a professional tool, but I have not taken advantage of what it can do just yet.

Social Media Tools

Each social media tool has advantages and disadvantages, depending on what someone would like to accomplish with the tool and whom they want to communicate with. Here are my perspectives and insights about these social media tools.

LinkedIn

I'm an early adopter of LinkedIn. I was the 23,531st person to sign up, and now there are more than 200 million LinkedIn users. While I didn't really know what I was getting into when I signed up for it, I quickly found that LinkedIn is a great tool to stay in touch with the people I wanted to network with. Once LinkedIn started gaining critical mass, it really began to make a difference to my networking.

As of this writing, LinkedIn is the top business-oriented social media tool. However, things change rapidly online. LinkedIn could continue to be the top social media tool for business for years to come, or it could be replaced by another tool. Regardless, it is less about the tool itself and more about using the tools that are used by your peers and people who need to know about you. Tools can (and will) change, but the importance of networking never changes.

Corporate Social Media Tools

Networking is as important inside an organization as it is outside. Visibility, brand, and approachability are all important.

At Stanton Chase International, we use Yammer as our internal social media tool. As a global organization with over 70 offices in 46 countries, staying visible and connected is key to making a difference to our clients and our careers.

You may have your own internal social media tool. Spend time figuring it out. Contribute, and make it part of your networking plan.

Twitter

This short-message communication tool has become very popular, yet in my experience few senior finance people spend time on it.

Facebook

This is a very popular tool, but its value is more for personal use than professional. Should you be on Facebook? This is a personal choice. But the business case for being on Facebook for a professional has not been made yet.

Google+

I'm not a big fan. While everyone with a computer has used Google to search, and almost everyone has a Google-branded email account (@gmail.com), I have not found it to be a good networking tool. It does have some very powerful tools on it (my favorite is the video tool), but it has yet to gain traction for business professionals. But don't discount Google+. It may surprise us both.

Other Tools to Keep in Touch

Social media is generally thought of as the types of tools just mentioned. However, the following tools are "social" as well as "media." Any tool that allows you to stay in touch and visible with your network is an effective tool.

My most important recommendation when trying to reach others is: Know how your contacts like to communicate and respect their boundaries and time.

Skype

Skype is a powerful communication tool, and it is very effective if you need to communicate internationally. Recently purchased by Microsoft, this tool is replacing MSN Messenger. Skype is a very effective instant-message tool, as well. Most don't think of Skype as a social media tool, but any tool that allows you to stay in touch with your network is effective.

SMS

SMS is better known as *texting* in North America. Texting is continuing to gain traction in North America as a popular communication tool among business professionals. SMS has been very popular outside of North America for years. SMS is not a pure social media tool, but it allows you to stay in touch. I have used texting to communicate quickly and effectively with clients and candidates on search mandates when the information was brief and time was of the essence.

Email

Email should not to be overlooked, but no one likes spam. Gaining permissions with email is very important and so is brevity and clarity. Email works best when it transfers information. Email can cause misunderstandings if used as a tool to communicate lengthy or emotional detail.

Telephone

You're busy. You have things you need to accomplish. The telephone is the most time-intensive communication tool that exists other than meeting in person. Scheduling a time to talk with others can be more effective than just calling a busy professional and expecting that she has time in her day for you. Do you like your day to be interrupted by an unexpected phone call? Neither do others.

Separating Business and Personal Online

One of my CFOs mentioned that he uses Facebook for his personal life and LinkedIn for his professional career. This kind of separation between business and personal is important.

There used to be an expectation that our lives were personal and private. The world has changed, and it can be very difficult not to leave digital footprints of your personal life and professional career for years to come.

If you need privacy in your life, I do not recommend becoming a CFO. You can become a lightning rod in the role of a CFO. Expect to get noticed.

It is also important to keep in mind that what you put out on the web can follow you forever. Whether it be a Facebook "like" to a comment, a photo that was taken when you were relaxing on vacation, a video that you created for fun, or something you've said speaking in public, it may come back to haunt you.

On this note, take the following precautions with social media.

- Think about what you want to say. What you put out may never be taken back.
- Think before you press Enter. Then think again. Not all your thoughts or ideas need to be shared with the world.
- Create a separate personal space for friends and family online that others do not have access to without your permission.

One example that should be known to all CFOs is the case of Francesca's Holdings former CFO, Gene Morphis. Morphis was fired in 2012 for cause by his employer because he Tweeted information about his company that should not have been made public.

Another CFO who was fired for inappropriate social media use was Adam Smith, former CFO of Vante Inc. Smith gained national attention with an online video in which he berates the CEO of a retail outlet over his view about gay marriage.

These former CFOs will no longer have the opportunity to work as a Chief Financial Officer.

SKILLS DEVELOPMENT

Professionals can only be at the top of their game if they continue to learn and grow. Identifying what areas you need to continue to develop is essential to continued career success.

You can't be a master of everything. You need to focus and specialize to be successful. What skills do you need to be successful? What skills does your team need to have to support you with the skills you don't have?

To know what skills you need to develop, you need to identify what skills you have as well as the level of those skills. Next, you need to know what skills you will need as you continue to grow in your career.

Some skills that you may need to focus on to grow your career are:

- **Management.** How good of a manager are you? Are you hands-off or hands-on? Knowing your style is important, as it sets the stage for ensuring your delivery.
- **Interpersonal.** It is easier to criticize someone else's interpersonal skills than it is to scrutinize our own. How well do you get along with people? What situations do you do well in with others?
- **Negotiating.** *Yes* is the hardest word to get someone to say. Are you good at getting people to *yes*? Learning negotiation techniques is important for finance professionals as they move toward an executive role.
- **Technical.** Finance professionals start their careers focusing on technical issues. As they continue to move up the ladder of responsibility their need to be technical decreases. Yet it is important to be on top of technical issues, because at a senior level, you are looked upon for your input on these matters. How to continue to be technical enough while moving toward the strategic is a challenge that many CFOs and future CFOs face. At a senior level, awareness of technical issues, or knowing what you *don't* know, is more important than knowing the issues in depth. Are you surrounded by or do you have access to technical experts, both internally and externally? How can you deal with technical challenges you have never been exposed to before?
- **Communication.** How well do you communicate? Do you recognize verbal and nonverbal cues in others? Do you recognize them in yourself? Can you present your ideas in a room of 10 people or 100? How good are you at listening and asking the right questions? Do you know when to be quiet?
- **Relationship.** To accomplish as a CFO, you need to manage many different and sometimes competing relationships. How do you meet everyone's expectations of you? Can you manage the political game? Relationships are key to success at your employer, and will be addressed at length in Part Two of this book.
- **Business knowledge.** This is one of the most critical yet least-focused-on areas for skills development for the corporate finance professional. The company relies on the CFO and his team to provide information and insight as to how to meet financial objectives. Yet, how many finance people really understand the business they are in? Do they understand what drives revenue and profitability? Can they teach others in the business how to approach finance issues and make better business decisions?

I asked my CFO advisors what three skills they felt they needed to develop to become a better CFO. Three of the most popular answers were:

1. Communication
2. Financing
3. Relationship

What are your top-three skills for further development?

1. _____
2. _____
3. _____

 ## CAREER COACHING

Career planning is not an easy process. Doing it alone without any input can be an even bigger challenge. Where do financial professionals go to get help with managing their careers?

Career coaching is not a new concept, but over the past decade it has come to the forefront of ongoing career development at the executive level. There are even career coaches who specialize in helping CFOs with their careers.

One popular CFO coach is Cindy Kraft. Kraft works one-on-one with senior financial executives to help them position themselves for career success. She says that in her experience, "senior finance executives are best positioned to start career coaching at least 9 to 12 months in advance of thinking that they would like to make a career move." While Kraft says that CFOs are best positioned to start career coaching well in advance of a move, she believes that "CFOs who plan in advance are the minority."

I asked my CFO advisors if they had used a career coach in the past. While 42 percent said they have worked with a career coach at some point in their career, 86 percent agreed that they would benefit from career coaching.

Here are comments by my CFO advisors on the benefit they feel they would gain working with a career coach.

> The biggest benefit is to put a formal action plan on paper that should be continually updated during your career and monitored against your progress. If it's not in writing, it's just a dream or a vision.

I'm not sure what to expect from a career coach, so not sure
whether I would benefit.

How to improve career prospects and become more capable for my
next position.

To think beyond my current position and be accountable and plan
for my career growth.

I have been fortunate to have strong mentors and peers in my
inner circle, so I have not needed a career coach per se.
Whether I would benefit from working with a career coach is
a different story.

Some people confuse career coaching and executive coaching. Kraft says
that "career coaching focuses on building a career to the next logical move
within reasonable expectations, while executive coaching looks at what needs
to be done internally to be successful and effective" at your employer. We will
discuss executive coaching for the CFO further in Chapter 7.

Confusion also exists around the word "coach" because it is often inter-
changed with "mentor." As an executive coach myself, I have spoken with
different coaches, both career and executive coaches, who have trouble
describing the difference between a coach and a mentor.

So what is the difference between the two? A coach is a person whose
interest is to be disconnected from your current reality, allow you to see things
from a different perspective, guide you, and advise you. Most importantly, a
coach will give you homework. A mentor will allow you to discuss your
thoughts, but you have to be the driver.

Coaches get paid for their services. Mentors do not.

A mentor can provide you with guidance and feedback. A coach keeps
your goals and objectives clear and ensures you stay on the career path you are
seeking.

CONCLUSION

- We established that career success requires a plan.
- We discussed the value of knowing your technical and personal strengths
  and building upon them.
- We explained what a personal brand is, how it helps with career success,
  and how to build your brand.
- We discussed the importance of investing in networking before reaping the
  career rewards it provides.

- We reviewed the most popular social media tools for CFOs and provided tips for using social media effectively.
- We identified that continued skill development is key to continued career success for the CFO and provided examples of areas that CFOs should focus on for maximum career impact.
- We discussed the benefits of career coaching for the senior finance professional, and the most effective time to look at career coaching.

Career success requires taking the time to think about your career. You need to know yourself, understand how others perceive you, develop positive relationships with people who can make a difference to your career, be visible, and improve yourself. Perhaps you can do all this yourself, and perhaps you can hire someone to coach you forward in your career. Regardless, efforts invested in your career will have an impact on you today and in the future.

CHAPTER THREE

Career Danger Signs

T HE CFO IS, IN many companies, the second-highest-paid person. Unless CFOs are independently wealthy or have scored a big win on equity in previous employment, they generally rely on their income to live a certain lifestyle. CFOs may be known internally for their frugal nature, and most often they live within their means, but until this senior finance professional is ready to retire, she counts on the income she is earning to live.

The recession of the late 2000s was a wake-up call for many senior corporate finance professionals. Too many CFOs found out the hard way that their careers could not be taken for granted.

Career CFOs are individuals who need to keep busy. When I speak to CFOs who are between opportunities, I find one of the most difficult issues they face is that they are not as busy as they were when they were working.

Irv Lichtenwald, CEO of Medsphere, became a CFO early in his career. One day in 2003, after much planning and preparing for an orderly transition, he retired. It was his choice, and he was looking forward to enjoying life.

He soon found himself bored and itching to be active again. One day he was having lunch with a friend who was an investment banker, and mentioned that he was bored. The investment banker friend then asked him to join a company his bank wanted to invest in. Lichtenwald has not looked back, and is now CEO of the company he joined as CFO.

I asked my CFO advisors what was their biggest fear about being unemployed. Here are some of them.

> I fear irrelevance as a professional and a person. Financial concerns are second.
>
> Having too much time on my hands and not enough to do is my fear. Most of us do not have hobbies as we were totally immersed in the business world.
>
> Not being able to provide for my family is my biggest fear. Also, there is a perception (right or wrong) that people who are unemployed must not be very good at what they do or lack significant skills. This hurts your job search.
>
> I fear the unknown. I have never been unemployed and I have significant financial commitments for my family. One of the biggest fears is having to move my family from a good community, school, and friends.
>
> My biggest fear is not being able to be employed at a similar or better position in my next role. I am also convinced that my opportunities will be fewer due to my age.

CAREER DANGER SIGNS

The likelihood of senior professionals being unemployed for a significant amount of time increases with the more years of work experience they have. This is a fact of life that too many CFOs do not plan for properly. The strategies in this book will have an impact on you personally if you take them to heart and realize that you are the only one responsible for your career.

While much of this book deals with career and employment strategies, let us take a look at some career danger signs that might be on your current career highway or on a road that you take in the future.

Exclusion from Meetings

The change happens suddenly, and you do not really notice when it starts. Until now, you have been in on all key meetings about the business. When you have not been involved in these types of meetings, you were either invited to attend and did not think it was necessary or you were not able to attend because of conflicts. At least you knew about the meetings and the topics, and usually got a briefing on what was discussed and agreed upon.

Now you are noticing that when you want to reach your CEO or your peers, they are in meetings. You did not know about these meetings, you do not know what they are discussing, and you get a feeling that something is going on that you should know about, but you do not.

Then it hits you. They are talking about you.

Distance

Since you started with the company, you have had an excellent relationship with your CEO and peers. They have been warm and friendly to you and you to them. You have enjoyed a camaraderie and playful, lighthearted friendship that transcended the day-to-day issues of running a business together.

You have begun to notice that the warm smiles you have received regularly are no longer given as liberally as they have been in the past. When you receive a smile, you question its sincerity. The best way to describe what you are feeling is that your CEO and peers are distant.

You realize that you are no longer part of the team, anymore.

Out of the Loop

You have always been in the loop. You have always been aware of projects and initiatives before they were made public to employees. You were part of these conversations from the beginning, and were included in the conversations about how to communicate these important changes to employees and outsiders.

One day you find out about a major strategic initiative for the company from someone else. This person may be your employee, who is asking for more information on how this initiative will affect him. You find yourself in a difficult position because you do not know how to answer your key team member and make an excuse to postpone the discussion. Or, even worse, you hear rumors about important news about your company from an outsider, like your banker or your supplier. This news gives you a "deer in the headlights" look that is hard to avoid.

Just like those signs on the highway that warn you to watch out for deer crossing, this is one more sign that your position is in danger.

New CEO

The CEO who hired you is no longer with the business. One scenario is that the CEO came to see you one morning to let you know that he was leaving for another career opportunity. Another scenario has you being woken up one Saturday morning by a phone call from the chairman of the board letting you know that they would like you to become interim CEO as the current one has been asked to leave or cannot continue for medical reasons.

Whether you have been appointed interim CEO or not, your position is in danger, unless you are made the new permanent CEO. The reason is quite simple. CEOs like to choose whom they work with. If for any reason the new CEO does not want to work with you as the CFO, you will be asked to leave.

Your only hope is that you can build an excellent and valuable relationship with the new CEO. Otherwise, your time with your current company is limited.

Limited Board Relationships

Your CEO likes to control the interaction between the board of directors and company management. The CEO has made it quite clear by his or her actions and words that you should not be speaking with board members or sharing any management information without it being processed and filtered by the CEO.

As a new CFO you could readily accept this arrangement. You were hired by the CEO, with limited board interaction, which makes it clear that the CEO is your boss. Being new, you do not question how things work at your new employer. As time continues, you realize that you are not communicating and building relationships with the board. There is no opportunity for them to learn about you, your capabilities, and your professionalism. Everything they know about you has been told to them by the CEO.

One day, the CEO says something to you that you know in your gut is not right. You cannot imagine that the board members are aware of this initiative, because if they were, they probably would not agree to it. You would like to have a confidential discussion with one of the board members, yet your CEO does not allow you to speak to them directly. You do not even have a relationship with one of them that will allow you to have the kind of conversation that will be unofficial yet provide you with guidance and input on how to best manage a difficult situation.

You are stuck. You fear you are being made out to be the fallguy. Even if you find a way to deal with this situation, you now realize that it may be time to leave before being asked to do so.

Integrity and Ethics

Senior finance professionals are very ethical people. They are proud of their ethics and integrity and make decisions regularly that need to pass through their own ethical filter.

Yet CFOs and other financial leaders find themselves from time to time in situations where they are asked to do things that may not pass their ethical filter. It might be a method of accounting for a transaction or reporting of an event for tax purposes. It could be a situation in which a supplier is treated unfairly, or one that is not even-handed in its treatment of an employee.

The Sarbanes-Oxley Act was a reaction to unethical business behavior that was uncovered at the turn of this century. The legislation required a lot of additional compliance work at public companies to ensure that they met the letter of the law. Yet the spirit of the law required that there be a proper "tone from the top"—not only that senior management, starting with the CEO, asks that employees act ethically, but that the CEO and other senior managers do so as well.

One of my CFO advisors noted, "Working with senior executives willing to live in a gray area is a slippery slope." Another advisor felt that working with management and a board that lacks integrity can put your career in jeopardy.

It is better for you, as a corporate finance professional, to leave a business where ethics is a challenge than find yourself marked with a stain of ethical impropriety that can severely limit your future career.

Mergers and Acquisitions

North American business culture puts a premium on continued growth. When growth is being asked for and organic growth will not be enough to fuel the requested growth, mergers and acquisitions (M&A) is a popular option.

I would venture to say that there is not a corporate financial professional who has been working for more than five years who has not had a merger or acquisition affect his or her career. In my first job out of university, I joined an accounting firm and before I even started, it was acquired by Ernst & Young.

CFOs and other senior finance professionals are important players in M&A. A key component of M&A work is the finance aspect. Finance is involved in identifying and helping to value potential acquisition targets, performing financial due diligence, as well as the integration of the financial systems and reporting after being acquired.

When acquiring companies that are smaller than yours, there is a lot of opportunity for the finance team at the acquirer. When your business merges with or is acquired by another one, positions, including the CFO's, can be at risk.

There can be only one corporate CFO. If your company is acquired, it will most probably not be you.

Cash Flow

Overall success in a business hides a number of underlying problems that can afford being swept under the rug. When a business is successful and cash is not an issue, the job of finance in a company is relatively easy. When a business is facing operational and financial difficulties, Finance is at the forefront of getting the best value of available cash while trying to increase available cash for survival.

As leader of the finance team, you are asked to make the best out of a difficult situation, and sometimes you are asked to perform miracles on a daily basis.

Cash can only stretch so far. At some point, the company may not be able to afford to keep a highly compensated CFO like you.

Financial Markets

Public companies have advantages and disadvantages. Some of the advantages of being public include increased brand awareness and visibility as well as having more options when raising capital. Disadvantages to being public include the high cost of compliance and a tendency to have a short-term business focus because of share price fluctuations.

When you are a public company, financial markets have an impact on your share price. Public company CFOs are well aware that they look good when the company stock price is high. They also know that when the share price is at an all-time low, they bear a lot of the stress—and might even be held responsible.

Whether public or private, difficult financial markets put more restrictions on what tools CFOs can use and the price they can use them at. When financial markets are difficult and you are restricted in what you can do to make a difference to the company, your position might be in jeopardy.

Scapegoat

Bad things happen to good businesses. Sometimes the issues are small and can be overcome. There are situations where mistakes have happened because no one can be perfect 100 percent of the time. Companies are not islands. There are things that happen outside the company that can have a significant negative impact on the business. It can be one big bad thing or the perfect storm of many smaller bad things.

Finance reports on operational and business success. When the CFO reports good news, whether internally to employees or to the board, CFOs have told me that they are just seen as the reporter, not the cause. However, when the CFO is the bearer of bad news, she or he bears the negative feedback personally.

Bad news can make the CFO feel like a scapegoat. Too much bad news can actually turn the CFO into a sacrificial lamb.

Stagnation

Ask any finance professional what company was the most exciting one to work for, and he will most probably mention a company that was growing. Companies in growth mode are thrilling places to work. Increasing sales, new locations, continuous hiring, new product launches, and the smell of fresh paint make working in a growth company fun.

When a company is stagnating, the fun disappears. Sales are flat or decreasing, locations are closing, staff is leaving, there are no new products, and the paint is peeling. The business is no longer a fun place to work.

Change is a constant in the business world today, even if you work in an environment as stable as government. Many companies are in a situation where things are stable, so why would they rock the boat? Stagnation is a sign that while things may look like smooth sailing, the boat is taking on water and the captain doesn't even know it.

CFOs working for companies in stagnation should keep in mind that one of two things will happen. The boat will sink, or they will be thrown overboard.

Boredom

CFOs need to watch out for boredom setting in. A number of my CFO advisors mentioned boredom as a career danger sign. If you're a future CFO reading this, you might be asking yourself: "How could it be possible for a CFO to be bored?"

I do not believe that boredom is a danger for all CFOs, but it can be for some. It can be found more often in companies that are facing stagnation than those that are in growth mode.

Starting out in a role, a CFO cannot be bored. There are too many new things to learn and understand, from how the company makes its money to who the key people are inside and outside the company. In many cases, a CFO is told that there is a specific area that needs fixing and is a priority when he joins the company. Once the problem is fixed and things are running smoothly, it begins to dawn on the CFO that the company that hired him may not really need a CFO.

This is when boredom sets in. Will the CFO leave, seeking another challenge, or will the company question why it needs a CFO in the first place?

The following danger signs have similar characteristics:

- ▨ Lack of challenge
- ▨ Complacency
- ▨ Loss of passion

Overwhelmed

I have never met a CFO who was not busy and who did not have a full plate. That said, there is a difference between being busy and being overwhelmed.

When a CFO has too much on her or his plate, something will fall off. In Part Two of this book, where we will be talking about CFO relationships, we will address how to manage the expectations of the people you work for so that you don't have too much on your plate.

Some CFOs get overwhelmed because they cannot say no to their CEO or their peers. They end up with special projects that are full-time jobs in addition to their primary responsibilities and do not shift any of the work around to others in their group.

Some CFOs need to do, touch, and know everything. They will never admit that they are control freaks, but this could very well be what the people that report to such CFOs think about them. Delegation is not a weakness, yet CFO control freaks worry that they cannot trust (and verify) the work that their teams do.

Whatever the reason for being overwhelmed, this danger sign can cause serious problems for the CFO and the company. Watch out!

CONCLUSION

- ▨ We know that CFOs are among the best paid executives at most companies, yet frequently face the risk of losing their jobs.

- We discussed that while in between job opportunities, CFOs not only face personal financial concerns but boredom, as well.
- We reviewed a number of signs that can spell impending career danger for CFOs.

CFOs have a responsibility to themselves to be aware of signs of impending career danger. Caught early enough and dealt with properly, these signs may help the CFO avoid career danger. If not dealt with before it becomes too late, CFOs will find themselves looking for their next opportunity with no incoming cash and facing potential boredom. Chapter 5 discusses strategies for CFOs who are in such a transition.

CHAPTER FOUR

Should a CFO Moonlight?

T HE SHORT ANSWER IS *yes*.

This answer might surprise you a little. I previously mentioned that Chief Financial Officers (CFOs) and senior corporate finance professionals take their jobs, responsibilities, and careers very seriously. Serious and responsible professionals do not moonlight. They should be completely dedicated to their primary role, shouldn't they?

This answer is *yes*, as well. CFOs and future CFOs need to be completely dedicated to their employers and their careers.

"So, Samuel," you are asking, "how can you call for complete dedication on one hand and advocate moonlighting on the other hand?"

CFOs who are dedicated to their employers and their careers must moonlight to be able to give their best to both.

Moonlighting gives you more visibility. It allows you to gain and improve skills you do not currently have. Moonlighting gives you the opportunity to meet new people and grow your network. All of these things have a positive impact on your employer and your career.

Does that mean you should leave the office early, take long lunches, spend the day on the golf course, and be unavailable for days at a time?

PERCEPTION IS REALITY

There is a potential downside to spending time on projects outside your direct employment. People may think that you are not pulling your weight. This perception can be a problem if not managed properly.

A bigger issue can be that you are so busy with outside projects that you do not have enough time to deliver what you need to in your CFO role. How can you bridge the gap?

It is important to communicate the value of your extracurricular activities to your CEO, board, and employees. They need to understand and accept that there is value accruing to the business by the work you are doing over and above your role. You need to help foster a culture of giving and involvement in outside pursuits within your finance team as well as help set the tone with other executives. It's hard to be the visible chairman of a charitable initiative in a company that has a culture that discourages this.

ACCEPTABLE MOONLIGHTING METHODS

When I say *moonlighting*, I do not mean playing hooky (although hockey might be acceptable). To me, moonlighting means dedicating some of your time and efforts to things that are not directly related to your work but have an impact on you career and your employer.

I asked my CFO advisors what kind of moonlighting they did. Figure 4.1 shows their responses.

Volunteering

There is tremendous value in volunteering. Many professionals who give of their time to a cause they believe in say that it gives them great satisfaction to make a difference.

When I assess profiles of executives for a position, those with involvement outside of their employment get extra points. Few companies are looking to hire a selfish CFO. Businesses want to see well-rounded individuals who can look beyond themselves and understand what it means to be part of a community. Volunteering looks good.

But there is more to volunteering than just "looking good." Being part of a volunteer effort in name only does not add value to you or your employer. You need to be actively involved.

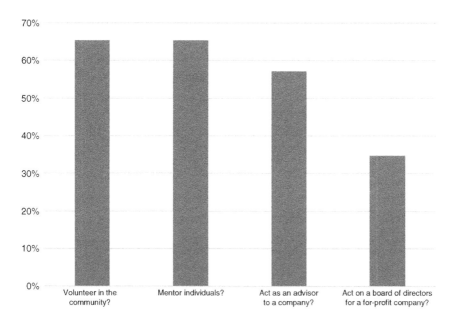

FIGURE 4.1 Types of Moonlighting

Should you use your time when volunteering to accomplish for the community effort, or should you use it as a personal opportunity to build skills, gain experiences, and build your network?

Both giving and receiving value is appropriate when volunteering. You need to feel that you're making a difference. People who volunteer usually say that they get more out of it than they put in.

While being active in volunteer work is important, it is important to pace yourself and set limits. I have seen too many people (myself included) get caught up in the high that comes from being too involved in your community.

Volunteering can be a significant commitment for the busy finance professional. It is important to ensure that you feel you are gaining and accomplishing from the efforts. You do not want it to have a negative impact on your career or your family and personal life. You want to make a difference but not burn bridges.

Benefits of volunteering include:

- Meeting people outside of your professional or personal circle.
- Having an opportunity to work as part of a team with others whom you would never work with.

- Challenging yourself.
- Feeling good.

Pitfalls to be aware of in volunteering include:

- Not managing time properly.
- Not meeting commitments—your word is your badge—will be remembered and can be detrimental to your brand, even in a nonpaying environment.

When I asked my CFO advisors to explain why they volunteered, here are some of the answers they gave.

> Volunteering helps me remain grounded and humble.
>
> Anything that brings in fresh ideas is something I find helpful. It is really a philosophical thing. I believe that you get what you give. Many people helped me, and I feel it is one of the best ways to give back.
>
> Broadens perspective and increases networking opportunities.
>
> I don't do it for the benefits. Contributing is satisfaction enough.
>
> Benefit from meeting new people and getting exposure to new issues, solutions, and ideas.
>
> Volunteering has provided me with an opportunity to give something back. It has also provided me with personal development, allowed me to create loyalty, and in some cases has created useful contacts.

Volunteering has provided my advisors with personal satisfaction, skill development, and networking opportunities. You can gain these advantages, too.

Mentoring

Each of us has had a mentor in our careers. Sometimes the mentorship was formal. Other times it was informal. We may not even be aware when we are mentoring or being mentored; it can just happen naturally and without a plan.

Mentorship can be provided to people in our own companies, or it can be provided to those who work elsewhere. Value accrues to you regardless of who the person is or what company he or she is working for.

Mentoring certainly has more of an impact when it is formal. The ability to make a difference in someone else's career can be satisfying. But most mentors realize that mentoring others also helps them. Pointing out areas for improvement and career growth to those who come after us can help us figure things out for ourselves. This benefits our careers as well as our employers.

My CFO advisors had the following to say about mentoring.

> It feels good to help others feel better about themselves as they move toward their goals.
>
> It helps build leadership skills.
>
> I have mentored several young employees and interns in this role and past roles. I find it to be a very productive way to reflect on my past successes and failures navigating through my career.
>
> It is my responsibility to develop people in the organization and prepare them to become the next generation of leaders here.
>
> Mentoring people provides me with an opportunity to help others better understand and consider what their end goal is and how to focus on this.

Two out of three of my CFO advisors have been mentors to others. They gain valuable insight and enjoyment from this activity. You can make a difference to yourself and others, as well.

Advising Other Companies

Small businesses have the ability to become big businesses, and some eventually do. Yet, according to the U.S. Small Business Administration, half of all new small businesses fail within the first 5 years, and only one-third of them survive past 10 years in business.

Advisors to smaller businesses, whether they are just starting up or have been in business for a while, can have a significant impact on these companies.

I consider advising to be an informal type of consulting. As a corporate financial professional, you can provide yourself as a sounding board to other businesspeople on an irregular or infrequent basis and still make a difference. You don't need to commit to a deliverable, but you can provide an ear and some valuable ideas. It's as simple as spending time talking with a business owner.

What value do corporate financial professionals gain from talking with business owners about their businesses if they get no compensation?

Many CFOs enjoy being involved with businesses other than their own. They love learning about different businesses and learning from others. They also like to be asked for their advice.

CFOs find that they are asked for input and guidance from business owners and others in a nonbusiness setting. Almost like doctors, CFOs and future CFOs get asked how to cure business pain.

There are CFOs who actively seek out opportunities to make a difference to other businesses. Some CFOs find themselves acting as advisors to businesses without planning to—it just happens. Regardless whether they seek opportunities to advise companies, or whether entrepreneurs seek out their advice, corporate financial professionals who help others in business help themselves.

I have been told by a number of CFOs that their being active and visible in their local business communities has been excellent networking for them. Not only has this added to their brand and visibility, but it has helped CFOs find new suppliers or customers for their employer as well as provided them with access to excellent career opportunities.

Advising other companies is something my CFO advisors find valuable. Here is what they have to say about being an advisor:

> Broadens perspective and increases networking opportunities.
> Adds value to a start-up company that they otherwise would not have had.
> For the most part, it is about my desire to help others with my skills and giving back.
> My current CFO position began as a part-time advisor to a start-up company.
> When I help a small business, I can't help feeling I'm MacGyver— I'm building something from nothing.

More than half of my CFO advisors have gained value from advising other companies. Consider increasing your visibility and brand by doing the same.

Board Directorships

The board of directors is the holy grail of CFO moonlighting.

Serving on another company's board of directors is a significant commitment that can be the equivalent of a part-time job in addition to your full-time job as CFO. Often board members are paid for their time in cash and stock incentives. CFOs need to make sure that they have the buy-in and approval of their employer to be on the board of another company.

Board positions in not-for-profit organizations certainly add value to you, your employer, and your career. I consider these positions to be volunteer roles and not in the same league as for-profit directorships. My discussion about board directorships here does not include not-for-profit roles.

One out of three of my CFO advisors said they have been directors of for-profit companies. This statistic seems, from my experience, to be a little higher than I would have expected it to be. CFOs do also serve on the boards of the companies they work for, so this may explain the discrepancy. Outside North America, the CFO is also often called the Financial Director (FD), and FDs sit on the boards of directors of the companies they serve. In a North American context, this situation is less common, but it does happen. The board positions I am referring to here are nonexecutive positions with companies other than your employer.

Things to consider before joining an outside board include whether competitive issues exist that might affect your employer and whether you can properly deliver on your commitment to both your employer and the company on whose board you serve. The last thing you need is for this additional commitment to prevent you from delivering what you need to your employer or to the company of which you are now a director.

Why do I believe that a board directorship is an ideal moonlighting opportunity for a CFO?

With CFOs most often being the right hand to the CEO or the second in command at the company, they need to interact with their boards of directors. CFOs who are on the boards of other companies get to learn firsthand what being on the other side of the table is like, and they can learn a number of things that will help them become better CFOs. The insight gained from how a board of directors manages its corporate governance role ensures that you do a better job delivering to the board that you report to.

It is my experience that CFOs who have good board experience are usually top-notch CFOs. While not always the case, a full-time CFO with one or two board positions is generally a powerful and well-rounded CFO. I firmly believe that being a board member makes you a better CFO.

Board directorships are also excellent opportunities for the retired CFO. I have seen retired CFOs end up on the board circuit as a way to keep active, involved, busy, and making a real difference, as well as earn a living post-retirement.

The most popular position for CFOs on the board of another company is the audit committee. CFOs need to deal with the audit committee at their place of work, so sitting on the other side of the table allows them to gain amazing insight into how to do their full-time jobs better, all the while adding strong value to the boards they sit on.

There is another way that being on the board of another company can benefit your employer. For example, many banks have executives of key business customers on their boards of directors, as it adds value for them to know what their key customers are thinking. On the flipside of the coin, the bank's business customers also gain from being involved with the bank's governance.

The biggest challenge in becoming a director of a for-profit company is similar to the challenge of becoming a CFO for the first time. Just as it is hard to be a CFO if you have never been one before, it is difficult to become a director for the first time. Once you have been a director of a for-profit company, you are more likely to continue to be considered for these interesting and sometimes lucrative roles.

The most common way to become a first-time director is to network your way into the role. Being part of a circle of people who serve on boards is an effective way to eventually be asked to join this exclusive club.

CFOs who are interested in success should consider adding outside board experience to their resumes. It will not only enhance their career opportunities, it will have a significant impact on them becoming better CFOs.

 ## CONCLUSION

- ▪ We identified that moonlighting outside of work can have a positive impact on your employer and your career.
- ▪ We spoke about volunteering and the benefits that you are receiving when you are giving.
- ▪ We mentioned mentorship and the importance of contributing to the development of other professionals inside and outside the company.
- ▪ We discussed the benefits CFOs gain when they advise other companies.
- ▪ We reviewed the value to the CFO and her employer of the CFO being a member of a board of directors for another company.

As we grow in our careers, we are led to believe that we need to give all of our efforts to our employers. Spending time on projects that are work-like but not directly related to the work we do can have a significant impact on our careers as well as our employers. Doing something different has many personal benefits, which should not be overlooked. CFOs need to realize that focusing only on their careers is preventing them from being the best CFOs they can be.

CHAPTER FIVE

The CFO in Transition

M OST CHIEF FINANCIAL OFFICERS (CFOs) can expect that there will be times in their careers that they will be in between jobs. Following the strategies in this book will reduce your risk of unemployment, but will not eliminate the potential of this happening to you.

CFOs are generally not well prepared for the transition process. They are great at what they do, but when it comes to looking for a job, they find themselves in a job that they have not trained for. Not only are they not prepared to look for a job, they usually do not enjoy the process, which makes it even more difficult for the stressed, unemployed, former CFO.

Many senior corporate financial professionals have always been able to find work quickly in the first 15 or 20 years of their career. These people have never had to look for a job for an extended period in the past—the opportunity always found them. Then, one day in their 40s or 50s, they find themselves in a situation they never imagined: unemployed.

THE GRIEVING PROCESS

Becoming unemployed is a personal loss. This situation can have a real impact on the person's self-esteem in addition to creating financial concerns that need to be dealt with. In my experience, many if not most CFOs are not properly prepared for unemployment. The loss they feel may not be equivalent to that felt at the passing of a loved one, but it is still a loss that can impact a person's well-being.

Grief is a process. It does not just happen after the job loss. Grief has an impact over the life of the transition period until the next career opportunity is secured.

Following is a list of the steps of grief, and how they impact the senior corporate financial professional in transition.

Denial

Senior finance professionals can find themselves in denial when they find themselves in transition. The most common denial takes place when CFOs begin to see the warning signs indicating their jobs are in danger but continue to act as if their employment is secure. Another common denial is that once they know that they will no longer be employed, they refuse to accept that their new job is transition. They need to work very hard to ensure they do not stay unemployed for too long.

Anger

Unemployed CFOs can be an angry CFOs. They may be angry at their previous employers for not treating them right after their complete and full commitment to the company. They may be angry when they realize that they are no longer needed. Anger can be directed at family, friends, colleagues, and even themselves.

Bargaining

This part of grief is the "if only" stage. If only I were a better CFO. If only I had worked harder. If only I had negotiated the funding. This is the part of the rationalization process that allows the CFO to move along in her grief when no longer employed.

Depression

CFOs who have been in transition in their careers are very aware of this stage of grief. Depression can be present in the beginning of a transition. I have certainly seen it in those CFOs who have not been able to find a job within a decent amount of time. Depression can be a challenge for the CFO in transition for the simple reason that future employers will not be interested in a CFO who cannot be positive and happy during the interview process.

Acceptance

CFOs in transition who are able to get to this stage are fortunate. The sooner they get to acceptance and realize that they need to focus and accept their situation, the sooner they will be able to get to the hard work involved in finding their next CFO opportunity.

If you have found yourself in transition in the past, these stages of grief may sound familiar to you. If you have been fortunate enough to not have been in transition yet, be aware that grief will take hold of you. Grief of some sort is inevitable. How you manage it will impact the effect that grief will have on you. Taking the following steps to manage your transition and move beyond this period of your life will allow you to minimize the impact of the grieving process.

 WELCOME TO YOUR NEW JOB

You now have a new job. Whether you are a CFO who has made the decision to move on from your current employer or you are a CFO who has had the decision made for you, your new job is looking for your next job. You may be a great CFO, but that does not make you a great job seeker. As a matter of fact, if you are like most of your peers, you are probably not very good at it.

You find yourself in this new job that you don't want, are not prepared for, and are not qualified to do properly. Yet, you need to do great work in this job to be able to get back to the job you love.

A question I am asked constantly by CFOs in transition is: "How is the job market for CFOs?"

From my perspective, the state of the regional, national, or even global job market for CFOs is irrelevant to your job search. This job market is the macro-level market. The question that you need to ask is at the micro level. How is the job market for *you?*

As a CFO in transition, you only have to make one sale. You are not a mass-produced product. You are unique. You have a mix of knowledge, skills, and abilities that few can really compete with, because there is no other CFO like you. However, be very aware that when a company is looking for its next CFO, it isn't necessarily looking for you. It might be, but the chances are against it.

This assessment sounds grim. As a numbers person, you should know that the numbers do not work in your favor. Without properly tackling your new job as CFO in transition, your probability of finding an ideal opportunity for yourself is unattractive, indeed.

This is a good time to remind you that CFO success can only be achieved if you focus on your employer as well as your career. It is also a good time to mention again that most senior financial professionals do not give enough attention to their careers while employed.

If you have been paying proper attention to your career all along, I can *guarantee* that should you find yourself in transition, your period of transition will be shorter. You will have more career choices and better career options than if you did not focus on your career all along.

If you have not been building your brand and visibility and nurturing (feeding) your network when you were employed, you have to begin from scratch. You can do it, but realize you have a lot to catch up on, and it will cost you time, and perhaps opportunities, as well. It is important to note that those who have put appropriate focus on their career on a consistent basis rarely end up in transition because excellent opportunities find them before they end up in a situation where they are looking for their next career position.

IDEAL STATE

The ideal state of a CFO in transition is *not to ever be in transition*. In this ideal state, you have already developed your brand, you have visibility, and your network has been working for you all these years. You have built brand, visibility, and a network *before* you find yourself without employment. When you invest in your career consistently, great opportunities will find you first. The best prepared CFOs will rarely be without great career opportunities before stepping away from their previous positions.

If you have nurtured your branding, visibility, and networking throughout your career and you do end up in transition, at least you have the benefit of having your ducks all lined up in a row. You can hit the ground running. You will be able to reconnect personally with your network, and your contacts will be happy to hear from you and willing to go the extra mile to make additional introductions. You are steps away from having excellent career opportunities coming your way.

 ## CATCHING UP FROM BEHIND

If you are not in an ideal state, all hope is not lost. Thankfully, you can take an active role to decrease your time in transition and increase your chances of success.

Where should you start?

Outplacement Services

If you have been referred to outplacement services by your previous employer, you should make sure that you get the most value out of this parting gift. Too many professionals in transition fail to exploit this important benefit.

Not all outplacement firms offer the same type of service, and differences in style certainly exist. Your outplacement specialist may not give the same advice that I give. These differences are minor in the end. Any assistance that you get that helps you move toward your goal of getting your next position is beneficial.

Action Plan

You need to have a plan. One of the key benefits that CFOs in transition get from outplacement services is guidance and coaching on how to create a job search action plan as well as the discipline of having to report to someone to ensure you keep to your plan. If you do not have outplacement services, you will need to work harder to ensure you make your plan and keep it.

This is not one of the times in your life that you can wing it. As CFO, you certainly need a plan of action for your employment, which we discuss in Chapter 7. It is also important to have an action plan for your transition process. You may have been trained to become a CFO, but you did not train to become a CFO in transition. You may know how to act as a CFO instinctively, but you are not aware of how to act instinctively as a CFO in transition.

Your plan should identify:

- What your next job should look like, including details on the roles that will most suit you, the environment that you want to work in, as well as compensation and location requirements that are realistic while meeting your needs.

- Your daily schedule, including what you need to get done every day, the hours you will work in this new job, and what you will *not* do during work hours.
- The people you have met with and spoken to, including dates for follow up and people they mentioned whom you should speak with.
- Targets and metrics. Know how many people you will need to meet and speak with and ensure you meet your goals.

Time Wasters

There are a number of things that professionals in transition do that are not effective and can be considered a waste of time. Here are three things CFOs in transition should not spend too much time with:

1. Resume
2. LinkedIn
3. Recruiters

Resume

Yes, your resume is important. Those with access to outplacement services will usually have assistance with preparing a resume and should take advantage of the help. As a CFO in transition, it is important to have a solid resume that summarizes your experience and gets the right messages across to the reader.

Unfortunately, many finance professionals in transition spend too much time on their resumes. Making your resume a continuous work in process does not help you get out of transition faster. I have seen people waste their time doing and redoing their resume, getting feedback from everyone they meet. In the end, they have a resume that does not properly represent them. They also find that they wasted time on their resume when they could have met with people who would put them in front of others who may have the opportunities they were looking for.

A resume is your brochure. To get hired in your next role, be aware that your resume is only marketing material. You still have to sell your way in to the right opportunity for you and then close the deal. A resume can only help you so much. Spend more time prospecting and selling, and less time worrying how pretty the marketing material is.

LinkedIn

Chapter 2 discussed the value of LinkedIn for career development. I am certainly a big fan of LinkedIn. Yet LinkedIn is only a networking tool. LinkedIn does not replace networking; it supports it. I recommend that a CFO in transition be on LinkedIn and properly use it as a networking tool. I strongly recommend that you limit the amount of time you spend on LinkedIn daily, because otherwise it will suck up a lot of your time and prevent you from being effective in your search.

Recruiters

Recruiters are thought of by CFOs in transition as *the* people to know, because recruiters have lots of jobs they are looking to fill. I am a retained executive search professional who is very visible in social media with a focus on CFO and senior finance positions. Because of this, I have a number of CFOs in transition who reach out to me and want to talk to me. My time is limited and I try to find the time to speak with as many people as I can. As someone in a relationship business, I enjoy investing in the careers of senior corporate financial professionals.

While I enjoy the conversations, the number of CFOs I speak with compared to the number of mandates I am working on does not work in the CFOs' favor for finding them their next opportunities. I certainly work to provide value and advice to each of the CFOs in transition that I speak with. However, unless I am already working on a search mandate that matches the profile of the person who reaches out to me, I will not be able to directly help him get out of transition. On the balance of probabilities, CFOs in transition who reach out to me are not going to find a career opportunity with me or any other recruiter they reach out to.

Recruiting professionals who are experts in finance are worth speaking with, but I would recommend limiting the numbers of recruiters you reach out to. It may be counterintuitive, but remember, executive search consultants work for their clients. They do not work for you. My experience has shown me that CFOs in transition have more success by networking effectively than by chasing busy recruiters.

Areas to Focus On

As mentioned previously, an effective CFO in transition is the CFO who is no longer in transition because she has found her next opportunity. Time wasters mentioned previously are areas that too many CFOs in transition focus on, believing they are being effective. Here are three areas that CFOs in transition need to focus on and spend time on:

1. Branding
2. Visibility
3. Networking

Branding

Chapter 2 discusses personal branding. When you know your brand, you understand how people perceive you. As you search for your next position, knowing what your brand is will allow you to explain your value proposition to the people you are networking with and the people who express an interest in the possibility of bringing you on board.

The best time to perform a branding exercise is when you are employed and effective in your CFO role. As a CFO in transition, you may not be in the best situation to perform all the steps to properly understand your brand. This should not stop you from doing homework to better understand how you add value to others. Understanding yourself better will allow you to sell yourself better.

If you need to catch up and better understand how to make personal branding work for you, I recommend reading *The Power of Personal Branding for Career Success* by Karen Wensley, published by the Canadian Institute of Chartered Accountants, 2012. The book and the accompanying online worksheets are an excellent resource to get you started. If you feel that coaching is needed, I highly recommend working with a career coach like Cindy Kraft (www.cfo-coach.com) who understands the specific challenges CFOs and future CFOs face.

Visibility

Opportunities cannot find you if you are not visible.

You need to be visible. You need to have an effective and current LinkedIn profile at an absolute minimum. Your LinkedIn profile needs to detail the roles you have been in, the companies you have worked for, and the branding statements that allow people to know what your value is. Your LinkedIn profile should also have a professional photo so you can be easily remembered.

Networking

Chapter 2 discussed networking tools, tips, and strategies. If you have not properly developed your network previously, you need to go personal and deep. Effective networking means having conversations that are, if not face to face, then at least voice to voice.

Networking when you need a job is not the best time to network, because effective networking is not about you, it is about the value you can add to others. When you're looking for a job, it really is about you. To get your network to work for you, you need to work for your network first.

The conversations you need to have are about adding value. When speaking with people, ask questions and listen. Understand what is causing them to lose sleep, then come up with solutions to their pain and communicate how you will make it all better.

I have spoken with CFOs who are part of transition networking groups who support each other during their transition process and provide each other with leads. One CFO in transition I spoke with brings a copy of my *CFO Moves* blog, (www.cfomoves.com), which he calls the Dergel List, to each of his meetings. Continuing to develop your "whom you know" will have deep impact on others who will return the favor to you.

HOW CFOs FIND THEIR NEXT OPPORTUNITY

I asked my CFO advisors how they found their previous role as chief financial officer. Two-thirds of them found their last CFO job through a referral from their network. A quarter of my CFO advisors were hired through a recruiter who contacted them, and the remainder applied online for opportunities.

Networking is the most powerful and effective way for CFOs in transition to find their next career opportunity. Those in transition who are actively networking are those who are playing the numbers most effectively in their favor.

Step away from your computer and get out there. Networking is where you will find your next CFO role if it does not find you first.

ACCEPTING YOUR NEXT CFO ROLE

Being unemployed can be an advantage and a disadvantage as you work to secure your next CFO position. You are at an advantage because if an employer wants to bring you on board, you can start almost immediately, which in certain situations can be very valuable to your next employer. However, a CFO who is currently working is more desirable to a company than you are as an unemployed CFO.

After working hard in your role as CFO in transition, you will start to get results. The people you meet with lead to interviews that will lead to job offers. Being desired by a potential employer is great news for a CFO in transition. There are issues that you need to be aware of while you are in the offer process. Things to consider include:

- Fit
- Location
- Due diligence
- Multiple opportunities
- Gut check

Fit

This is something that is overlooked too often by CFOs in transition. Senior finance professionals tend to spend more time looking at whether they can do what the job description asks for rather than whether the potential employer's culture and environment is really good for them.

Location

I have found CFOs in transition to be more open to relocation than CFOs who are settled in their roles who are approached about another opportunity. Being unemployed usually means few options will not be considered. I have followed too many situations where CFOs were hired and then left because of family and personal complications that arose after the fact that had them move back to their previous locations.

Due Diligence

CFOs do not like surprises. Yet most CFOs only know what they got themselves into once they have been in the CFO chair for a bit, and then it can be too late. CFOs need to act like investors once they are interested in an opportunity. For CFOs who understand financial information very well, reviewing financial statements and budgets, both on a global basis as well as for the main business units, will allow for a better understanding of the operations. It will also allow the CFO to ask key questions of the potential employer.

Multiple Opportunities

As mentioned earlier in this chapter (Welcome to Your New Job), you only need to make one sale. If you have done a good job during your transition, you will have more than one opportunity. Managing multiple opportunities is an enviable position to be in, but it can complicate decision making for the CFO. You need to ensure that the decision you make will be the best one for you and your family. I recommend that you look at the opportunities and be honest with yourself as to which opportunity would be best for you *before considering compensation*. Money aside, which is the best opportunity for you? Once you answer that question, put compensation back into the equation and see if you have the same response.

Gut Check

Before accepting any role, you need to feel comfortable that the decision is right for you and your family. Your instincts have been developed over years in your career, and now is the time to trust your gut. You could be wrong, but to start a new role, you have to not only be interested in it because you need the money or are bored in transition, it has to be because it feels right. Can you be passionate about the position? Are you excited? You need to be. If you're not, try to understand why before saying no to the opportunity.

 NEGOTIATING YOUR NEXT EMPLOYMENT CONTRACT

You have done your transition job well, and you have piqued the serious interest of a potential new employer. They would like to make you an offer for the role, and you are interested in accepting. How do you ensure you get what you need from this new opportunity?

My blog, *Samuel's CFO Blog* (http://blog.dergelcfo.com), has discussed this topic in the past, and it continues to get traffic based on people looking for advice on this important subject. The advice that I'm giving here is not legal advice, but practical guidance on issues for CFOs to consider when negotiating their agreements with new employers.

In any negotiation, you need to understand what you need, and what the person or people you are negotiating with need, and see how you can get to a comfortable situation where everyone wins. You need to finish negotiating when you are (mostly) satisfied and your future employer is content. Know what is important to you and what is less important to you. Understand what your future employer can and cannot do for you in the area of compensation. Keep an open mind, listen, ask questions, and negotiate professionally. Be very aware that your future employer wants a CFO who is a strong and fair negotiator. Here is your chance to show them that they are making the right hiring decision.

If you are interested in examples of employment contracts, in the United States you can look at 8-Ks filed with the Securities and Exchange Commission (SEC) of publicly listed companies (www.sec.gov). Most countries with public stock exchanges have similar filings. For Canada, you can see company filings by visiting www.sedar.com, and in the United Kingdom, you can search on www.londonstockexchanges.com. These filings include employment agreements of actual CFOs for real companies with complete information. It can be very helpful to find real examples, but be aware that if you will be accepting a CFO role with a publicly listed company, the complete details of your employment can be available for your neighbor, children, or ex-spouse to look up, as well.

Base Salary

This cash compensation is what CFOs are most interested in. It is the basis of what they take home after taxes and other deductions and could be the basis of other compensation items like bonuses and other benefits.

All CFOs want more money to take home. They care about this number very much. The challenge most CFOs have when it comes to understanding and accepting what this number should be is that they base what they want on what they earned in the past.

CFOs who are currently working who get recruited to another role are at an advantage when negotiating base (and other compensation items), because they can successfully argue that they will need to give up their four quarters and are not interested in a dollar bill.

CFOs who are in transition believe themselves to have the same power in negotiating as their peers who are employed, but they are incorrect. A CFO in transition is earning a round number, otherwise known as zero. They are not in a position to be strong in negotiating base compensation and other benefits.

CFOs need to understand that their earning potential is limited by the earnings of the CEO and other key executives. CFOs will never earn more than the CEO, but could be the second highest earner in the company. If you are being hired by a public company, do your research on securities filings to get the picture of key executive compensation. Know what current executives are earning and what executives have earned in the past. Know where the previous CFO stood on the compensation ladder relative to the CEO and other key executives. Understand who the company's direct competitors are and what their compensation looks like.

If you are about to be hired by a private company, asking for this information is possible. If you do get hired, you will know pretty quickly what the CEO and other key executives are being paid. The last thing a company will want is a CFO who knows he was hired with compensation that does not compare properly to other key people in the organization. Sharing this information, as well as making a reasonable offer based on this information, is important to the company hiring its next CFO.

Knowing how the CEO and other executives in the company are being paid provides you with the basis for finding a reasonable solution to what your compensation, including base salary, should be.

Annual Bonus

Bonuses at your future employer may be paid in cash, in equity, or a combination thereof. Some companies pay bonuses to executives that are based on pure discretion. Others have a formula that is based on a mixture of company financial performance, meeting corporate strategic objectives, and personal performance. The bonus structure for executives at the company you are being considered for will be unique, yet will have some combination within these parameters.

It is important to gain a detailed understanding of how the bonuses at your potential employer are calculated and what that could mean for you. Once you understand how bonuses are paid out, you may be able to negotiate the percentages on which they are based.

Automobile

This benefit for executives can be a good place for the incoming CFO to negotiate. Based on your personal situation, you might consider negotiating for either a car allowance or a company-owned vehicle. While I do not recommend making this issue a major item, it can be a good place to seal the deal.

Expense Reimbursement

It is my recommendation that you have a clear understanding of what is appropriate and acceptable when it comes to expense reimbursement, especially in public companies or nonprofit or government organizations. Your agreement may refer to a company policy for expense reimbursement for executives. If your new employer has a policy, make sure you understand it clearly before agreeing to begin work.

I highly recommend that CFOs and senior finance executives negotiate a budget for professional development (PD), which could even include a professional development spending account. Continuing to develop your technical, leadership, and industry knowledge should be an investment your next employer is willing to make. Having clarity on this up front is most beneficial to a new CFO.

A PD spending account can include the ability to pay for traveling to and attending conferences as well as paying for executive coaching. Knowing what you can spend up front without having to sell the idea and get approval for each conference or coaching session gives you the flexibility you need to continue to build your career and add value to your employer.

Other expenses that can be included in this budget can be for items that are necessary for company business and personal development, including clubs, industry groups, professional dues (i.e., certified public accountant fees), and chambers of commerce. Charitable giving from the company to causes that are important to you can also be something that can be included in your agreement on expense reimbursement.

Relocation or Travel Assistance

Finding your next CFO role near where you live can be a challenge, especially when you are a CFO in transition and you need to expand your area of search to increase potential opportunities. In a number of situations, companies understand that they will need to provide relocation assistance to secure the best and most appropriate CFO for the role. In other cases, CFOs may not be able to relocate, but may accept significant travel to be able to serve their new employer properly.

It is important for CFOs to know whether a company is willing to pay for relocation or travel when beginning conversations with companies that are situated outside of the area they live in. If a company is not willing to consider paying for these costs, knowing this at the beginning of the interview process with a potential employer is very important.

The details of this assistance should be left to the negotiation stage. If the company is serious about hiring you as its next CFO, its offer should include an appropriate offer for relocation. This type of assistance should minimize or negate the cost to you of moving yourself and your family to a new location.

Sometimes it may not be possible to relocate immediately because of personal reasons. In this situation, particulars should be agreed to in advance, including travel schedule, budget for travel costs, and an agreement on when relocation should take place and how those costs will be covered.

Signing Bonus

Executives love the idea of a signing bonus. Before you get excited about the idea of extra cash for saying yes, it is important to understand the reasons why companies offer these bonuses to new executives.

I have seen signing bonuses given to make the offer more interesting for a candidate the company really wants to bring on board. A signing bonus is a sign that the company really wants you on board.

It can also be given to make a new executive "whole." CFOs and other executives who are being recruited from another company might have to forgo an upcoming bonus that they will no longer get should they leave the company, and a signing bonus can be a way for the new employer to ensure that the executive does not suffer by accepting the offer. Signing bonuses may also be given because a new CFO may be in a situation in which he needs to repay a certain amount to his previous employer.

The situations where a signing bonus makes sense mostly apply to CFOs who are working before accepting a new position. For CFOs in transition, it would be rare for a new employer to be convinced that a signing bonus is appropriate and necessary.

Health Insurance

In today's business environment, having appropriate and sufficient health insurance for executives is a necessity for companies wanting to attract top talent. It may be difficult to negotiate the details of an insurance program that applies to all executives, but it is important to be aware of what this important benefit offers.

For a finance executive in transition who may no longer be covered by employer-paid health insurance, getting covered as soon as possible can be an essential benefit. If there is a waiting period as part of the insurance program for new employees, ask the company to get the waiting period waived. This can provide the CFO in transition with a valuable short-term benefit.

Death or Disability

We live our lives as if every day were not our last. Just as certain as life happens, so do death and illness. Having clarity on what happens should you not be able to make it into work is important for you and your family. While there may be standard executive insurance policies for these issues, you should know what happens with your compensation if illness or death occurs.

Should you face a serious long-term illness and not be able to return to work, it is important to be aware how this can impact your continued coverage for health insurance for yourself and your family.

It is common for companies to take out life and disability insurance policies on their key executives to manage risks and costs of such an event for the company. I recommend that if your company does this for its key employees, you should negotiate to have the option to take over the policy at your cost once should you find yourself no longer employed by the company.

Time Off

CFOs work very hard. Even if they do not work 24/7, their commitment to the company certainly is. Having scheduled and agreed upon time off is important to ensure you stay on top of your game.

You should get what other executives in your new company are getting when it comes to vacations. Hopefully, they give their executives an appropriate amount of time off. If this is really important to you, you could attempt to negotiate additional time. However, there are generally better places to focus on in your negotiation.

Annual Review

Be aware what the company policy is for your official annual review. Be sure that the company has a policy and sticks to it. This formal process for feedback gives both you and your manager (likely the CEO) the opportunity to ensure expectations are managed and issues are dealt with.

Termination

If you are like most of the finance professionals I speak with, you are interested in job security. Unfortunately, the only place I have seen the existence of any form of job security is in someone's head. Change in the business world today is a constant, and job security, even for senior financial executives, does not exist.

It is important to understand that the chances of your remaining with your new employer for an extended period of time (i.e., more than five years) are slim. With this in mind, let us take a look at what you can do to reduce the risks to you upon your eventual departure from your new employer.

For Cause

You do not want to be in a situation where you are terminated for cause. It is important for you to understand what actions can result in a termination for cause, if only to be sure that you never give your employer a chance to terminate you for cause. I have not seen many such terminations, but they do happen. And should you find yourself working at a company in the public limelight, being terminated for cause will have a significant negative impact on your future career prospects.

Without Cause

This is a very important area for you to be familiar with before accepting any new employment as CFO. You know you may not stay forever at your employer. Be sure you are well protected. Make sure that you will receive a significant severance package at the end of your employment if the company chooses to let you go without cause.

You may not know how many months of salary would be appropriate as compensation should you be asked to leave. I recommend that you speak with a lawyer who is an expert in executive compensation to ensure that you are getting what is appropriate in your market and legal jurisdiction.

It is also important to have detailed in your agreement what happens with bonuses, equity, and other benefits once you have been terminated.

Resignation

Today you are managing the issues related to accepting a new employment offer. You realize that you will not be staying forever, and that one day down the road you may wish to leave on your own accord. It is important for there to be an understanding as to the details of what will happen when you leave, including how much time you will need to give as notice.

Change in Control

In today's business environment, many companies do not continue in their same form over long periods of time. While many larger companies continue to exist, thrive, and even grow over the long term, most growth companies exist as an independent company for a relatively short period of time. Successful growth-oriented companies become targets for acquisition and takeover by larger industry players with more access to cash. Companies in high-growth markets that are struggling to accomplish their objectives often attract private equity firms that focus on restructuring the business or acquiring similar businesses to build a profitable niche. Businesses that have been in families for generations can be ripe for new owners to join and continue the business into the future.

These are some of the reasons why companies will have new ownership. New owners typically replace most or all of the executive team. CFOs need to prepare for this possibility as they negotiate their terms for their new employment.

Often, CFOs will be treated more generously when a change in control happens than when they are terminated without cause. In many cases, cash severance payments will be increased, cash bonuses will be paid, and equity awards will vest earlier than scheduled.

It is important to understand your benefits and rights should you be terminated following a change in control. You may want your agreement to not only cover an actual termination but situations where your responsibilities or compensation are reduced or altered.

Change in Strategic Direction

You sign on as CFO with a company that is aiming for an initial public offering. You are excited about this because you bring a lot of value to the table for taking a company public. Your agreement with your new employer states that you will be compensated significantly once the company actually goes public. One day you are meeting with the CEO and she informs you that the board has decided to postpone going public for the foreseeable future.

This is one example of a change in strategic direction that can significantly impact a Chief Financial Officer.

 ## CONCLUSION

- ▪ We reviewed the stages of grieving and how this process impacts the CFO in transition.
- ▪ We spoke about how CFOs in transition need to treat their unemployment period as if it were a job. Their new job is to work hard to find their next paying job.

- We discussed that the ideal state for a CFO in transition is to never be in transition in the first place. This can only be achieved by being branded, visible, and networked throughout your career.
- We mentioned that CFOs in transition need to take advantage of out-placement services if offered, prepare an action plan, avoid time wasters, and focus on branding, visibility, and networking. CFOs do not get hired sitting behind a desk.
- We identified five items to consider when accepting your next CFO role.
- We discussed areas that CFOs need to consider when negotiating their new employment contracts.

CFOs have been trained to become great CFOs. CFOs in transition have never been trained to have full-time jobs looking for their next jobs, and need to learn how to properly and effectively do so. CFOs in transition learn a lot about themselves when unemployed, and they should take advantage of what they have learned in the process. The branded, visible, and networked CFOs are in a good place to have career opportunities find them instead of having to look for their next CFO roles.

CHAPTER SIX

Starting Your New CFO Role

ONGRATULATIONS! YOU HAVE ACCEPTED a new Chief Financial Officer (CFO) role. You're excited about the new opportunity, yet a wave of anxiety is about to hit (if it hasn't hit already).

How do you ensure that you will be successful in this new role?

Traditionally, a new President of the United States is given 100 days in office to get things in order before being held accountable and responsible. You, too, as a new CFO, will generally be given a window to get started until you, too, are held accountable and responsible. Whether the number of days used is 90, 100, or 180, the number is less relevant than the fact that you have a honeymoon period.

How you get yourself started during your first 100 days sets the tone for the remainder of your term. You will never be able to get back the ability to start over in your CFO role. Now is the time to properly plan and prepare for how you will accomplish the great things that are expected of you with your new company.

ONBOARDING

The process of properly starting off at your new employment is known as *onboarding*. You may be fortunate to receive onboarding coaching and assistance from your new employer that can help you get started out of the gate effectively and efficiently. If you have not been offered this assistance, you will need to get this done by yourself.

When I asked my CFO advisors if their employers provided them with onboarding support when they started their last CFO role, only 24 percent said they received some type of onboarding assistance. My CFOs commented that most of the onboarding assistance they received was more informal assistance from the CEO, board, and other executives at the company to help them get comfortable and up to speed.

If you are like most CFOs, your previous onboarding was informal, as well. This being said, I cannot stress enough how important proper onboarding is to ensure a successful stint as CFO at your new employer. You cannot afford to wing it. A book that can help you get all your ducks lined up in a row to ensure onboarding success is Brand, Check, and Pedraza's *The New Leader's 100-Day Action Plan: How to take Charge, Build Your Team, and Get Immediate Results* (John Wiley & Sons, 2011). The book includes downloadable forms and tools that can be very helpful in bringing order to the chaos that can exist when starting a new executive role.

From my perspective, here are steps for properly onboarding yourself as the company's new CFO.

Before You Accept the Job

Your onboarding process needs to start before you get the job. As a matter of fact, it needs to start when you begin interviewing. When interviewing, you should begin to think like the CFO of the business you are interviewing for. Not only is this helpful for you if you get the job, but it is also a very good way to become CFO of the company you are interviewing for. You should act as if you're the CFO *before* you get the job. Identify the issues facing the business. Discuss potential plans of action for the important issues during the interview process with the key decision makers, especially the CEO and the board. Show the decision makers in the hiring process that you can do the job they are looking to fill.

Before accepting the job, you should know *what* you need to know as well as *whom* you need to know. Work hard to understand the expectations of the key people you will be working with. Knowing what others expect and developing an action plan to deliver on these expectations will allow you to start your next CFO role with the knowledge of what needs to get done.

You need to be comfortable that you are making the right choice to join the right company for you. Doing this homework before you accept the job can give you the added benefit of knowing as much as possible about the people and company you will be working with before you make the decision to join.

Once You Accept the Job

If you have the luxury of time before your first day, start putting steps into place so that you can start your first day running. As an executive, you cannot afford to wait a week from your first day until you have the tools necessary to start being effective.

Ask for your technology tools before you start. Get your laptop and email up and running. Get access to the financial information and tools so you can familiarize yourself with information that will be critical to your job.

Do not spend your first day getting settled into your new office. See if you can arrange to get your office set up before you walk in on the first day. The first day sets the tone. You can never have another first day.

Ensure you have clarity on the expectations of the people you will be reporting to. Understand what their priorities are for you to accomplish and the timeframe in which they must be achieved.

Meet with as many of your executive peers as possible prior to starting. Have informal meetings to learn about the people you will be working with and what they do. Understanding their expectations and how you can help them will give you critical information needed to put your plan together.

Begin to get to know the people who will be working for you. As with your peers, these informal conversations will begin to build the relationships that are necessary to gain the support you need to have the best finance team possible.

One excellent recommendation from *The New Leader's 100-Day Action Plan* is that you can ask to have your official start day be later than your actual start date. This will allow you to get work done and meet with key people before you must be at your desk with your team and peers watching your every move. It can also give you paid time to get yourself up to speed so that you're ready to roll on your official first day.

Vision

You are not only the new leader of the finance group, you are a leader among your new peers. You need to have clarity on how you see your role in supporting the business. What is your vision of finance within your new business? How do you see finance supporting your CEO and your peers in making the business succeed?

Building this vision and getting buy-in from your team and support from your peers will be essential to your success at your new employer. The best way to build this vision is to draft it yourself. Before communicating this plan in its entirety, it is important to gain feedback and input from key leaders on your finance team as well as learn what your business partners will need from you to be successful.

You can only be successful if you know where you want to go and have the buy-in of the people who will help you get there. Once you have a clear vision, you will need to communicate this to your team and peers. Your team members will need to buy into your vision and live it. Your previous experience tells you that this is not easy to accomplish, yet you know in your heart that having a vision will allow you to accomplish great things. Show your leadership and act on it.

Know the Lay of the Land

If you are new to the company, there is institutional memory residing within the company that you do not have. This puts you at a disadvantage to others within the company who have this institutional memory.

Know the Business

Understand how the company makes money (or should be making money). Familiarize yourself with the company strategy. Understand what the opportunities are for the business and the corresponding challenges. The better you understand the business, the more effective you can be in making decisions and collaborating with others in your business.

Know the People

As mentioned previously, technical skills can get you only so far. The more you know the key people in your business, the better you can manage those relationships. Part Two of this book will discuss the challenges of building these important relationships and how to succeed in getting the best out of these relationships. When you begin, the more you know about the official organizational structure as well as who makes what decisions and the influence these people have, the better chance you will have to start making a difference during your honeymoon period at the company.

Know the History

As the new CFO, you are focused on the future and changing things for the better. While you don't need to know everything that happened in the past at your new company, you do need to understand the history of success and failures. Your accomplishments will build on the past, and it is important to know what foundation you have inherited.

Early Wins

You need to impress upon the people who chose to hire you, as well as the people who have to live with the choice made for them, that you are the right person for the job. The best time to make an impact is during your honeymoon period. By making decisions that will have immediate impact, you show that you are getting comfortable with the company and the role, and you are staking out leadership within your company. Early wins allow you to show that you are making tangible progress.

This is not to say you should not focus on long-term wins, as these are very important to your success as a CFO. As the new kid on the block, you are being judged on what you can accomplish. The sooner you are able to achieve visible and meaningful accomplishments, the more secure your future will be with the company and the more seriously you will be taken by the people you work with. This, in turn, will pave the way for you to be able to get the support you need to get larger, longer term wins.

Team

As CFO, you can only be as good as your finance team allows you to be. CFOs need the support of a qualified, capable, and motivated team to give them the room to be successful. Chapter 12 will discuss building and developing the CFO's finance team in more detail.

When you start as CFO, you inherit a team and a structure. It is important to understand what you have inherited as soon as possible. Can the team you inherited help you meet the vision of what you want to accomplish in your new role? This assessment needs to be made fairly quickly, and the more information you have, the better decisions you can make.

The decisions you need to make include:

- What should the structure of your team look like?
- Will the current leaders you have inherited fit well into your planned structure?

■ Who should be asked to leave? Who gets promoted? Which roles should you hire from the outside?

Answering these questions will ensure you have the best leadership possible for your team.

You are the CEO of the finance group. You need to act like a leader. You need to connect with your people. You need a strategy for how your team will make a difference to the company and an action plan to meet that strategy. You need to get quick buy-in from your new team to support you in this effort.

Making team and people decisions are some of the most difficult things that leaders have to do. You need to make good decisions here, and you need to make them fast. Using logic rather than emotion is critical to setting yourself up for success at your new employer.

Process and Technology

When you first start as the new CFO, it is important to assess whether the processes and technology that you inherited will allow you to deliver on your commitments. In most cases, some process and technology will be lacking. In some cases, a lot will be missing.

If there is a lot missing, it is important to understand why process and technology have not been kept up to date. Speaking with your team members can provide you with an appreciation for what happened in the past that caused the lack of attention to and investment in these essential areas. If the reasons are mostly because previous finance leadership did not make this a priority, then you are in a good situation to make the necessary changes. If previous leadership made the effort to push this forward but was not able to gain the necessary resources, your job may be harder to accomplish.

Regardless of what happened in the past, you need to be able to secure the resources and internal support necessary to make the appropriate changes in this critical area. You should start with focusing on quick wins, as technology investments are not overnight projects. People, process, and technology are the key pillars of support for a successful CFO, and the sooner you focus on building those solid pillars that will support your vision, the closer you will be to securing your success as new CFO.

Attitude

You are the new kid on the block. You may have some tough decisions to make in the first 100 days, but you need to have a positive attitude to accomplish your tasks. No one likes a sourpuss. The challenges you face as new CFO will be significant. Preparing a plan and making things happen are certainly vital. Having the right attitude is critical to gaining the support you need to make the changes that are necessary to accomplish your vision for finance in your new company.

There are a number of different ways to ensure that you start off on the right foot in your new CFO role. The strategies recommended previously are important to ensure your success as you begin. You can complete all these strategies, follow the guidelines in *The New Leader's 100-Day Action Plan*, use another onboarding guide, or get direct onboarding assistance from a consultant or coach. Whatever path you choose to take to make yourself effective as a new CFO, you absolutely need to prepare a plan to make this new challenge work for you.

ONBOARDING EXPERIENCES OF REAL CFOs

You are aware that new CFOs need to plan their onboarding to succeed at their new employers. My CFO advisors shared their experiences of being new CFOs with me, and I would like to share their real-life experiences with you.

Getting Up to Speed

I asked my CFO advisors to share what they did to get up to speed as soon as possible. A summary of their most popular answers follows.

Meet Key People

The first thing that most of my CFO advisors did when they started was meet with key people inside and outside their new companies to better understand the business they had just joined. They prioritized whom they needed to meet and took action to meet with them either before they started or just after. Responses ranged from meeting the CEO, board members, and other executives, to site visits at key company installations, to speaking with outsiders such as bankers and auditors, in addition to meeting key members of the finance team. These meetings happened over lunch, dinner, and coffee, on-site as well as off-site, over the phone, or by videoconference. My CFO advisors made meeting key people a high priority and felt that this was an essential way to start out well in their new roles.

Review Documents

CFOs are analysis experts. Numbers resonate with finance professionals. Reviewing the numbers, recrunching them, and asking questions based on their research allowed my CFO advisors to go broad and dig deep. These reviews brought out opportunities to take advantage of and inconsistencies to learn from. My CFO advisors felt there was a lot to learn from such reviews and appreciated the opportunity to review this information as early as possible in the process.

Understand the Business

All organizations exist to add value. The questions that CFOs need to understand about their new business are, What value should the business be adding, and how does it go about adding this value? Their function is to support the value-add that the company has committed to. Whether joining a new industry or a new business within a familiar industry, CFOs need to understand the business before they can add value to the process. My CFO advisors took the time to challenge themselves to learn about the business they had just joined. Whether it was meeting with key people or reviewing documents, they took their roles as new CFOs seriously to ensure they were able to add value as early in the process as possible.

Biggest Challenges

Starting out as a new CFO provides numerous challenges. I asked my CFO advisors what issues they faced when starting out in their most recent CFO position. They shared their biggest challenges with me.

Adapting to the Culture

New CFOs have to adjust to the culture of the organization they have just joined. Sometimes the culture can seem familiar, and other times it can feel like they've entered the Twilight Zone. No matter what the culture is like in their new company, they need to adapt. CFOs need to take the time to understand the people, how decisions are made, and how to adjust their ways of getting things done to fit the culture of their new company.

Finance Team

One of the biggest challenges faced by my CFO advisors when they started was the finance team. Most of them needed to make some changes to their teams.

Some CFOs had to make significant if not drastic changes to the finance team. Regardless of what they had to do, they first had to understand the strengths of the people on the teams that they had inherited. These new CFOs met their teams, looked over previous performance reviews (where they existed), discussed the strengths and challenges of their team with others, and had to make the right calls quickly.

Learning the Business

Finance people understand business. Yet each business is different. When CFOs previously worked in the same industry, they only had to learn about how this company was different and unique. If the new CFOs came from outside the industry, they had to learn about the industry they had joined, with its quirks and challenges, in addition to learning about a new organization. Most of my CFO advisors spent a significant amount of time learning about the business by reviewing internal and external information, speaking with key people in the new organization, as well as traveling to different sites and business units. CFOs need to add value to the company as a whole as it goes about its mission. Understanding the business well is critical to helping the CFO meet this objective.

Financial Realities

I cannot say I am surprised that too many CFOs have been shocked by the financial challenges faced by the companies they have recently joined. When CFOs do not do their due diligence before signing an offer with their new employers, they will find surprises. Cash flow issues were the most common financial challenge facing the newly employed CFO. For some CFOs, the financial issues were fixable because they had the talent and experience to deal with these tough situations and overcome them. For other CFOs, these financial troubles persisted throughout their stints with their new companies. CFOs need to have clarity on the financial realities of the business before they agree to sign on.

Quick Victories

As mentioned earlier in the section "Early Wins," quick victories are an important part of successful onboarding. I asked my CFO advisors to share examples of their early wins with you. Examples of their most common early wins follow.

Relationship Building

New CFOs realized that building effective relationships with their board and CEO, executive peers, outside influencers, and their team was critical to their success in their new roles. These CFOs scheduled meetings, listened, and worked to understand how they could add value to their stakeholders. Taking the time up front to understand the needs of the people around them allowed my CFO advisors to take action and secure early wins. These wins allowed the CFOs to gain the trust of the people around them to continue to be successful in their roles.

Reporting

CFOs should always play to their strengths. Starting with a new company can allow CFOs to use their talent to accomplish quick wins. A common reason a company looks to hire a new CFO is that its old CFO was not able to give the company managers the information they needed to make decisions. CFOs with strong accounting and reporting skills should look for areas where they can quickly and easily make significant improvements. By combining these technical skills with understanding the needs of their internal customers, CFOs can quickly make a noticeable difference.

Cash Flow

The new CFO understands the importance of cash for the operation of the business. CFOs have years of experience in dealing with cash issues, from cash forecasting and management of cash to identifying and securing new sources for funding. This is one area where CFOs can rummage around in the bag of tricks they bring with them to their new employer and pull out skills, networks, and solutions that can have a quick, positive impact. New CFOs who help with cash flow early are appreciated and welcomed as key contributing members of the management team.

Analysis

This is one more area where new CFOs can build early wins based on their technical skills. Analysis can be done alone and without input from others, which makes it an ideal undertaking for new CFOs to begin even before their official first day. CFOs know how to read the numbers for the story they tell. The questions that arise from their analysis can be answered remotely or can be addressed in the first days of their employment. Combining an early analysis of information with questions allows CFOs to learn a lot about their new employers and how to make decisions that will have a significant impact early in the process.

Finance Team

When new CFOs have a vision for their team and gain an understanding of their true capabilities, they end up being able to make solid decisions that will support their tenure at the company. New CFOs need to invest time in meeting their team and understanding their strengths and motivations. They need to remove employees who will not be able to deliver, reorganize positions for those who can be more effective in another role, and fill the gaps by hiring the right finance leaders. CFOs who make these changes quickly after beginning show that they are in charge.

Changes Made

As discussed in Chapter 1, CFOs are unique. Their experiences are different, and the ways in which they approach challenges are varied. I asked my CFO advisors what changes they made when they began their new roles. Many of them made changes when they started at their new company; some found that it was not necessary.

None

Just because a new CFO comes in does not necessarily mean that there are changes that need to be made. In some cases, things are running smoothly when a new CFO arrives and he is comfortable with how things are getting done. However, I would caution CFOs to think carefully about keeping things status quo when they join a new company. Change is expected from a new CFO, and when no changes are made, this can be perceived as a weakness of character or skill that will not help the CFO be successful in the months and years to come.

Team

This was where many of my CFO advisors made changes when they started their new positions. Some made minor changes. Others made more comprehensive changes to their teams. These CFOs were acutely aware that their success was tied to the strength of their teams. They could not afford to have weak teams as this would make them weak CFOs by default.

Delivery

There is more than one way for the finance group to deliver support to the company. The CFO makes changes because she wants to have a service delivery model that makes most sense for the company. As an example, one CFO told me that he changed the structure of the finance team from having small groups focused on legal entities to a functional shared service model. Another CFO outsourced key non-value-add functions like accounts payable and payroll. These CFOs focused on adding value to the operations of the company and did not accept the idea that the finance group should continue to do things a certain way because they were always done that way.

Reporting

The company relies on internal reporting to make good decisions. External reporting is necessary for shareholders, lenders, and tax authorities. As discussed in the section "Early Wins" in this chapter, many CFOs are strong when it comes to reporting issues. Many of my CFO advisors made changes in this area because the companies they joined needed to make these improvements.

Starting Over

Hindsight is 20/20. Capable and intelligent people are able to look at the circumstances they are in and identify what they would have done differently had they known then what they know now. I asked my CFO advisors to share what they wished they had done before they started their new CFO roles, and their answers follow.

More Knowledge

When starting at a new company, people can never know everything about the company they have just joined. During the interview and acceptance process, a CFO candidate is being sold to. Selling is good, but some (or a lot of) information is not shared in the process. It takes time to learn about the environment you have just joined. My CFO advisors said they wished they knew more about what they were getting into before they accepted. This is not to say that they would have made a different decision, but a good number of them found themselves in situations that were surprising or uncomfortable. This is why CFOs need to do their due diligence before joining their next employer.

More Relevant Experience

You can get hired for a position without having all the necessary experience to deliver. Sometimes, new CFOs need to learn new things quickly and deliver on them. While CFOs are quick students, when facing something for the first time, it is normal to wish you had gained the experience previously. New CFOs do not want to look like they are winging it. CFOs are professionals who do not want to look like amateurs, especially when they know they need to impress in the first days of their new role.

Nothing

Some of my CFO advisors said that there was nothing they would have done differently. Confidence is attractive, and I believe these CFOs felt they did the best job they could given the circumstances they found themselves in.

Recharged Batteries

Many times, when companies are hiring their next CFO, they have needed to fill the position for a long time and are suffering without a CFO. They pressure the candidates they choose to start as soon as possible, because the need is great. CFOs want to meet the expectations of their new employer and try as much as possible to meet their scheduling needs. A number of my CFO advisors let me know that they wished they had taken a break and recharged. New CFOs who are tired and low on energy are not in the best position to make the greatest impact as they take on their new roles.

Negotiated Better

We discussed negotiating your employment contract in Chapter 5. The challenge CFOs face when they join the company is that they will quickly know how well they negotiated their package because they will have access to what others are getting paid in the company. When new CFOs learn that they are not receiving equitable compensation, it is hard for them to stay motivated. Such inequity can have a significant impact on the morale of the new CFO.

Biggest Surprises

Most surprises at work are not pleasant. Surprises that are caused by external factors are easier to accept than those that are caused because something was missed internally. When starting a new role, CFOs know there will be surprises waiting for them to deal with. The sooner they discover the surprises, the earlier they can fix them and move forward to the challenges that they were hired to deal with in the first place. I asked my CFO advisors to share the surprises they found when starting new CFO roles.

Controls and Processes

Sometimes a company looks to hire a new CFO because financial controls and processes are a known issue that needs to be addressed. When there is a surprise in this area, it means that either the company was not aware of it previously or senior management was aware but did not think it was important to mention in the interview process. Neither of these scenarios is pleasant. Regardless, the CFO needs to take quick and specific actions to address these issues; otherwise, they will be blamed on the new CFO.

Culture

This is one of the hardest things to really know about before starting because it is so intangible. Culture needs to be experienced to be truly understood. Some of my CFO advisors told me that they were surprised when they began to experience the culture, either because it was not the culture they were sold in the interview and acceptance process, or because they were told about the culture but were not able to truly appreciate how this would impact them.

Team

It can be hard for new CFOs to know what the teams they are inheriting will really be like. Sometimes the CFOs they are replacing built mediocre or poor finance teams. In other cases, the team was lacking the leadership necessary to be the best it could be. This is one area where new CFOs will only be able to truly understand what they have inherited once they start.

Cash Flow

Cash is king. Lack of cash can ruin businesses that have great potential for success. A number of my CFO advisors informed me that they only learned about the real cash and financial challenges that the company was facing after they accepted the offer and started work. There are reasons why this information was a surprise to the new CFO. It could be due to the ignorance of the company's leadership, who really were not aware of the cash and financial position of the company. Another reason could have been that the information was not disclosed to the CFO because it might have made it difficult for the company to hire a good CFO. The new CFO could also have not asked the right questions and made assumptions that were incorrect. Whatever the reason for this surprise, the CFO needs to take immediate corrective action to improve the situation.

CONCLUSION

- We introduced onboarding and its importance to new CFOs to ensure a successful stint at their new employer.
- We identified eight steps for the proper onboarding of a new CFO.
- We reviewed popular areas for the new CFO to get up to speed.
- We discussed some of the biggest challenges that new CFOs face.
- We mentioned areas that the new CFO can focus on for critical early wins.
- We spoke about the areas where new CFOs made changes soon after they were hired.
- My CFO advisors described areas they felt they could have done a better job on when starting.
- We identified areas where CFOs found surprises after they had accepted their new roles.

CFOs can be successful at a new company only if they are successful at the beginning of their tenures. Early failures can lead to early dismissal and becoming a CFO in transition once again. Starting out right in a new role is important for the CFO, and it does not happen without planning, foresight, and action. This chapter provided the new CFO with some insights on how to achieve success early and often. It is up to new CFOs to take the right steps for themselves and their new companies. The first 100 days are key to your success as CFO.

PART TWO

Successful Employment Strategies for the CFO

N PART ONE, I INFORMED you that CFO success requires a focus on your career and a focus on your current employment. Part One identified strategies for career success in each chapter.

You will notice that this book does not address technical proficiency as a key component of CFO success. As mentioned in Chapter 1, Bill Koefoed told us that strong skills in finance are necessary to do the job, but they do not differentiate you from others.

Your technical finance skills are an important part of what makes you a CFO. You need to have and use these skills as Chief Financial Officer. There are books, courses, conferences, and online resources that can help you improve your technical finance skills. Most of the training and development directed at CFOs is technical. There are some excellent resources available if you need to improve your mechanical abilities.

Part Two will focus on strategies to use with your current employer that will make you the best CFO you can be. These strategies include planning for success at your employer, managing your key CFO relationships, and building and developing the best finance team possible to support your CFO success.

You can be technically competent as a CFO, but if you don't have a plan, do not manage your relationships, and do not have the best possible team to support you, you are not destined to be a successful CFO for your employer.

CHAPTER SEVEN

Planning for Success at Your Employer

A S WE BEGIN TO discuss strategies for success as Chief Financial Officer (CFO), the best place to start is at the beginning.

Being CFO is the business that you run, not the business you work for. True, you are a critical component of the business you work for, but you are your own business. Your customer is the business you work for; you are compensated by the business you work for and have to deliver value for the business you work for. This requires a plan just as much as the organization that you work for. If you do not have a personal plan, you are planning to fail.

All CFOs will agree with this statement: Failing to plan is planning to fail. Yet, how many senior finance executives have a real plan for success? To answer this question, I asked my CFO advisors whether they had a plan for success at their employer (see Figure 7.1).

I am pleased that almost three-quarters of my respondents had a plan for employment success. What concerns me is that only 23 percent of my CFO advisors had a *formal* plan.

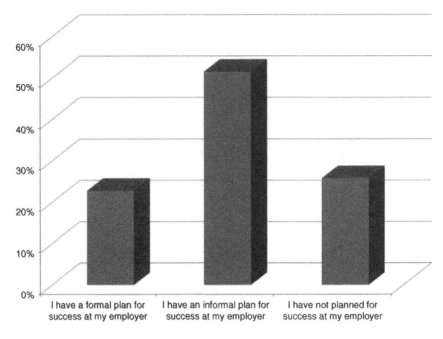

FIGURE 7.1 Do You Have a Plan for Success at Your Employer?

 THE CASE FOR A FORMAL PLAN FOR SUCCESS

Why should a CFO have a formal plan as opposed to an informal plan?

From my experience, Great CFOs create a written and formal plan for their success. Only through the process of writing it down can they keep themselves accountable by comparing what they actually did against what they planned to do.

Successful CFOs prepare their plans, write them down, review them, check their progress against the plans, and modify their plans as circumstances change and milestones are reached. These CFOs keep themselves accountable to themselves. This allows them to deliver the best value they can to their customer—the organization they work for.

CFOs who have a plan are able to be successful because they know what they are doing, when they are supposed to do it, and what their priorities are. This allows them to not only do a great job, but have the confidence they need to move forward with their plan. Others, including those you work for and with, and those who work for you, will notice your confidence. They will see your consistency and be grateful that you know what you're doing.

A plan for CFO success needs to be tied into the plan for corporate success. When CFOs understand what the corporation's plan for success is, they can adapt their plans to meet corporate objectives. It is important that CFOs be on the same side as corporate objectives, as their success ties directly into the success of the company they work for.

CFOs with a plan for success can decide to get input on their plan to make it even better and more realistic. In certain cases, it might make sense to share it (or parts of it) with your CEO or a board member. This could be an important part of managing expectations among the people you work for, which will be discussed further in Chapter 9: Relationships with the CEO, Board, and Investors.

Executive coaching is an excellent tool to help CFOs develop their plans and ensure that they stick to them. My experience with coaching CFOs is that they appreciate the opportunity to create their own plans for success at their employers and are grateful to have someone they trust who can keep them focused on their goals.

My CFO advisors commented on planning for success at their employers. Here are some interesting comments on the subject:

> I developed my own plan for success. Our HR organization talks a lot about talent recruitment, development, and management; however, it is mostly talk and little walk. If companies and senior executive teams spent more time developing and executing more formal plans, it would engage employees more into the strategy and its execution.
>
> Not sure what a plan for success is.
>
> My plan is constantly changing because my employer changes directions constantly.
>
> Due to chaos theory, my plan is always very light as I need to move quickly as the company changes course. I do ask my CEO and the board what success looks like. That keeps me from guessing.
>
> For all the areas that fall under my responsibility, I have a plan and goals to make them improve. Some are already successful and we are looking for minor improvements; some recently acquired responsibility areas have more significant improvement plans. All drive toward ultimate success.

Matching Finance Team Strategy to Corporate Strategy

It is important to understand the kind of business you are part of. Is your business a start-up? Are you in growth mode? Is your organization static, or is it in decline? Knowing where your company is in its lifecycle drives the strategy your business is moving forward with.

You do not want to be in a situation where the strategy for your Finance group is at odds with the business strategy. Finance team strategy that is misaligned with the corporate strategy can cause unneeded pain and suffering to the CFO, and may ultimately lead to his or her replacement.

The importance of aligning the strategy of the finance team with the business strategy was confirmed by 95 percent of my CFO advisors. While most CFOs agree that this alignment is important, many of my advisors have stories where strategy was misaligned. Table 7.1 details some of their experiences with misalignment and how they solved the issues they faced, or how they would have solved them as they look at the situations in hindsight.

This table provides real examples of misalignment and potential solutions to correct these strategic misalignments. Some of my advisors were not able to share examples of strategic misalignment because they never experienced any. Strategic misalignment can happen, but it does not happen at every company or for every CFO.

What is important to learn from these experiences is that strategic misalignment is possible, and that the CFO who wants to be successful needs to ensure that misalignment is identified (if it exists) and corrected.

Finance Team Culture

As CFO, you set the tone for the Finance group. Each company you have worked for in the past has had its own specific finance team culture. As leader of the finance team, it is your responsibility to set the culture (and change it if needed). In your previous work experiences, you may have seen the actual culture as different from the culture that was communicated to you during your interview experience.

Culture is much more than processes. The corporate failure at Enron was not about procedures not being followed, even if procedures were not followed. Enron failed because the culture was an "anything goes" environment, where corporate profitability was more important than ethics. Enron went wrong because of tone from the top.

TABLE 7.1 Examples of Strategic Misalignment and Solutions

Misalignment	Solution
We were investing in SOX readiness when going public was unlikely.	We should have waited until IPO was more likely.
At a former employer, the corporate strategy was driven by growth and innovation of new products and services with a very growth-oriented CEO. The finance strategy was centered on low cost as was moving much of its services to India in a cost-saving move. As a result, the finance team was not involved in the growth initiative, not included in decision analysis before an initiative was launched, and was frequently surprised to hear terms of a deal after it was consummated as the terms further complicated the financials and led to even slower monthly closes and reporting delays.	I did try to put a stop to the migration of work until we had stability in process, better alignment with the corporate strategy, and improved partnerships with the business teams.
Typically short-term objectives conflicting with long-term objectives. I was in an environment that was truly multinational, and we had to fit into the mold even though some were squares and others were circles; we all had to pretend we were triangles and compromise on certain levels. The Finance group globally was typically focused on cost. For example, it would deliberately postpone approval of CAPEX projects for months until cash flow positions were stronger or until we met their idea of a cost matrix for a project and met global KPIs [key performance indicators], so we missed out on a deadline for a major capacity expansion, which ultimately resulted in product being back ordered, not to mention missed long-term sales opportunities because of lack of capacity.	It is difficult to influence when there is a disconnect between global finance and local operations, especially when the head office has a "my way or the highway" policy. I moved on to another position because certain actions/positions asked of me went against my core values.
There was no corporate strategy and everyone was shooting from the hip.	I should have left the company earlier as they were not going to develop real strategic Initiatives.
The infrastructure was too fragile to support the rapid growth planned with the corporate strategy. We simply could not keep up in terms of staff skills, technology available, or processes in place. The finance team was constantly playing catchup to meet the demands, staff were burned out, and the growth plans could not be implemented as well as they could have been had the finance team been better aligned.	Build the finance team infrastructure ahead of the growth and take more risk on spending some resources to do that. Being too conservative when the rest of the company has a much higher risk tolerance was a problem.
Implementing a new enterprise resource planning system, while the company was up for sale.	Should have communicated this strategy to selected senior personnel, and not invested in the new project process, rather focused on the strategic initiative.

How do you create tone from the top? How do you work to ensure you set this tone properly, and that this tone is carried throughout your entire finance function?

Vision, Mission, Values

Creating the official culture of the finance team is important. Setting your vision for the finance team, detailing your mission, and explaining your core values is how you communicate what is expected officially. This can be done by creating a Vision, Mission, and Values (VMV) statement.

There is no right or wrong VMV statement. There is only a VMV statement that is right for your team and that fits the business culture you actually live in and want to live up to.

Living Your Values

If you identify your one of values as "We are honest and ethical in our practices," yet in reality you are not known to live up to this value 100 percent of the time, it will be difficult for this value to be taken seriously.

As the leader of your finance organization, you need to be a living example of the culture you are looking to create and perpetuate. Just expecting others to live up to your stated expectations without living your vision, mission, and values can create an environment destined for mediocrity and confusion, if not failure.

Goal Setting and the Path to Success

An important part of planning for success at your employer is setting goals. Your success as CFO is not only based on your personal success but the success of the finance team that supports you.

It is not enough to set goals; they must be SMART, which stands for:

Specific
Measurable
Attainable
Results-Oriented
Timely

When your goals are not specific, measurable, attainable, results-oriented, and timely, they are platitudes of hope, not goals that can be reached.

Personal Goals

I asked my CFO advisors to share some of their personal goals. A good number of their goals were SMART. Here are some of their personal goals.

Finance Core

- Improve financial reporting process and turnaround time.
- Develop a financial planning and analysis (FP&A) function.
- Consolidate and simplify diverse systems.
- Improve processes.
- Create or improve internal controls.
- Understand risks and prepare plan to mitigate them.

Operating

- Have a direct impact on improving operating results and shareholder return.
- Gain a better understanding of the business.
- Build relevant and valuable key performance indicators (KPIs).
- Have an impact on improving the supply chain.
- Reduce costs.
- Identify and support revenue increase and margin maximization.

Relationships

- Build credibility with outsiders, including investment community.
- Develop better relationship with CEO and the board.
- Become spokesperson for the company.
- Build trust with stakeholders.
- Become a true business partner to the operating units and departments.
- Build consensus and lead decision making.
- Lead innovation across company.

Financing

- Prepare plan for expansion.
- Access additional sources of financing.
- Prepare for/complete initial public offering (IPO).
- Make company attractive for investors or acquisition.
- Acquire companies and integrate them to increase revenue and profitability.
- Prepare an exit strategy.

Treasury

- Improve cash flow and management of cash.
- Develop effective strategy for short-term and medium-term investments.

Strategy

- Be more involved with the strategic planning process.
- Develop plan for increasing value of the business over the long term.
- Support strategic efforts in planning and implementation phases.

Personal

- Achieve personal financial success while at company.
- Exit company with $X.
- Prepare a personal development plan.
- Attend training.
- Hire an executive coach.
- Balance my work and personal priorities better.
- Acquire equity in the business.
- Delegate more effectively.

Finance Team

- Improve staff satisfaction.
- Prepare a development plan for the team.
- Build and hire for the team, increase depth of talent.
- Lead by example.
- Develop succession plan.
- Create a team that is versatile and can do multiple functions.
- Communicate better.

My CFO advisors identified these goals as most relevant to their situations. Can you identify your top-three personal goals?

Personal Goal 1: _____

Personal Goal 2: _____

Personal Goal 3: _____

Not only were my CFO advisors able to share their personal goals, but almost all of them (88 percent) told me that they had an actual plan to achieve these goals. When asked whether they actually keep themselves accountable to their goals, most (79 percent) said that they monitor and track what they do to achieve their goals.

When I asked my CFO advisors whether they monitor and track the actions taken to achieve their goals, I received these valuable comments to learn from:

> Setting and achieving goals can easily become interchangeable with company goals. Your questions have encouraged me to rethink my personal goals in order to establish some additional personal criteria for success. Thanks!
>
> We developed annual goals aligned with the business strategy. These annual goals were supported by very specific action-oriented trimester goal setting and reviews. The goals and results were always quantifiable and very specific.
>
> I keep a list of activities tied to each major goal or objective along with the start and complete date of those activities.
>
> Sometimes. Mostly I informally track in my head. Should do better at this, I know (maybe this should be one of my goals).
>
> My current goals are really out of date and are being recast as part of several sessions scheduled with an executive coach.
>
> My thoughts are this: When you write something down, you're thinking about it. If you share that list with others, you are more likely to hold yourself accountable to those goals because you know others know about them and may be relying upon you.

Finance Team Goals

In addition to setting goals for yourself as CFO, you must also establish goals for your finance team.

As CFO, setting your personal goals and achieving them will lead to your success. As mentioned previously, your finance team is key to your success as it supports you and ensures you are able to deliver on your commitments. CFOs can only be as successful as their finance teams allow them to be. Chapter 12 will discuss building and developing your finance team.

I asked my CFO advisors what their finance teams' goals for success were. Most of the responses were similar or the same as the list of their CFO goals. This should not be surprising. CFOs should want the goals of their finance teams to fall in line with the their personal goals.

If the goals for the CFO and the finance team are similar (if not the same), why should the finance team have its own goals in the first place?

The finance professionals who support the CFO need to be aware of what goals they need to reach for in support of the CFO. The CFO needs to set the expectations for the team so that there is clarity of purpose and knowledge of what the team, as well as individuals on the team, need to strive for.

A key part of getting the finance team to buy into their goals is to have them take part in setting the goals for themselves. Eighty-four percent of my CFO advisors told me that their finance teams have taken part in the setting of these goals. Here are some of their comments:

> The team has been an active participant in bringing technical team leaders up to speed with the financial management of their profit centers.
>
> I manage similar to a Servant Leader and prefer to have my team create their goals; then I vet them for alignment with company goals, add 10 percent to everything to stretch them . . . and off we go.
>
> Yes, they take part, but I steer.
>
> Taken part, reviewed, debated, and signed off on. Sometimes in teams with presentation to their peers, other times in full finance team sessions.
>
> As the CFO, I set the broad goals and put incentive dollars behind each goal and ask for their participation in placing the exact metric and details of payout.
>
> Goals are set by me and the controller. How they reach the goal is at their discretion.

While a good number (84 percent) of my CFO advisors told me that their teams are involved in setting their own goals, only 65 percent of them have detailed plans for achieving these goals.

As mentioned previously, having SMART goals (specific, measurable, attainable, results-oriented, and timely) is important to ensuring that your goals are not only known but achieved. As important as it may be to have SMART goals for yourself as CFO, it is even more important to have them for your team. Here are some comments provided by my CFO advisors on achieving team goals:

> We developed annual goals aligned with the business strategy. These annual goals were supported by very specific

action-oriented trimester goal setting and reviews. The goals and results were always quantifiable and very specific.

The plans continue to evolve and be refined.

Annual plan is broken down into 30-day priorities with metrics.

If needed, procedures to reach the goal will be put in writing in cases of longer or more complicated projects.

Detailed plans are part of their individual performance reviews.

Our team plan is more like a task list that establishes daily, monthly, quarterly, and yearly routines to keep us on track.

We have a detailed plan, but we're flexible, as well.

It is one thing to set the goals, and another to achieve them. A key challenge in meeting goals for team members is getting them to buy into the goals as individuals. I asked my advisors whether they felt their team members have bought into the goals, and an overwhelming majority (86 percent) said yes.

While almost all of my CFO advisors felt their team bought into the goals, I learned a lot from their comments. Here are some of them:

Joint ownership and individual "promises" statements from each finance associate regarding actions they will take to support the department and division goals.

Finance team bought in, but generating the understanding and acceptance failed at the CEO and board levels.

Overwhelmingly supported by my team because of the specificity of the goals, action steps, and link to the overall business strategy.

There is buy-in, but nervousness given various skill levels and places in careers. I am implementing dramatic change and change is scary. We need dramatic change to be successful— some people are excited and embrace change; others are more hesitant.

The buy-in is mostly driven by the incentive dollars and the fact that it is a stretch but reasonable.

Not sure—some acceptance, some on the sidelines.

The team has been committed to learning and improving since day one. The biggest challenge initially was the requirement for education and training. Once they were trained, they were very interested in taking on additional responsibilities and participating in meeting our goals.

EXECUTIVE COACHING FOR THE CFO

What is the first thought that comes to mind when you hear the word *coach?* When I hear the word *coach,* I think of the head coach of my favorite hockey team when I was growing up, the Montreal Canadiens. I can close my eyes and see Scotty Bowman behind the bench, chewing gum and whispering words (I can only imagine what he said) to Guy Lafleur and Larry Robinson. I see him pacing behind the bench and sharing his thoughts with the referee on a call he did not like.

In team sports, a coach is focused on the team rather than the individual. In a business context, a coach is focused more on the individual than the team. Executives, including those in the finance arena, are beginning to realize and take advantage of executive coaching as a means to become the best they can be.

You consider yourself to be a successful senior finance professional. You have done well in your career, and have always been able to meet the challenges facing you. You have never had an executive coach before. Why would you need one now?

The world is constantly changing. Markets, the economy, technology, customers, suppliers, and competitors are all changing regularly. The demands on the CFO from the CEO, board, investors, and regulators are also changing at a rapid pace.

The question is: Are you staying the same? To become the best CFO you can be and to stay ahead of the pack, you need a competitive advantage.

The good news is that most of your peers *are* staying the same. They continue to use what has been successful for them in the past in a world that is no longer the same. Your fellow CFOs are coasting their way out of the CFO chair. If you are ready to step up your own game, get yourself an executive coach.

As a CFO or future CFO, why would you need an executive coach? Let us look at five reasons why.

Plan

This chapter discusses planning for your success at your employer. Working with an executive coach allows you to work on your plan, get feedback, and keep yourself focused on your plan. If you want to plan and want your plan to succeed, working with an executive coach can only help.

Lonely

It's lonely at the (almost) top. I have come to this conclusion based on my discussions with CFOs over the years. Senior finance executives have told me that few people in their organizations understand the pressures they face, the complexity and the volume of the issues they deal with, and the difficulty of the conflicts they manage. While peer CFOs can be helpful in combatting loneliness, there are few people who can act as a sounding board and a guide on a professional basis. An executive coach can help keep the CFO from feeling lonely.

Relationships

The topic of relationships and how important they are to the success of the CFO, as well as how to manage specific relationships, will be dealt with in the coming chapters. When reading these chapters on CFO relationships, think about how much easier it would be to get the best out of these relationships if you were working with an executive coach who understands your work and your situation.

Feedback

As the boss of finance in your organization and one of the top members of the team running your company, you cannot expect to get the most honest feedback on how you are doing your job from your colleagues. At the top of the pyramid, there are very few people who will give you the constructive criticism you need to do a better job and improve. Senior finance professionals have told me that the higher they move up, the fewer people around them will tell them what they need to hear. Working with an executive coach can provide you with the candid and practical feedback you need.

Stress

Do you remember the days when you left your work on your desk at the office? They were probably a long time ago. Managing the stress of being CFO is difficult, yet it is critical that you do so. Expressing yourself and discussing what stresses you with someone who can understand the issues you face can go a long way toward actively managing your stress.

CONCLUSION

- We discussed the importance of a CFO having a personal plan for success.
- We gave examples of situations where the finance team strategy and corporate strategy were misaligned and instances of how those problems could have been solved.
- We identified how a Vision, Mission, and Values statement can help build the culture you want in your finance team.
- We spoke about setting goals for yourself and your team, and how they need to be SMART.
- We recognized the value of executive coaching and five reasons why a CFO needs an executive coach.*

CFOs are great businesspeople who need to remember to treat themselves as their own business. Planning for success increases the probability of it happening. Knowing what you need to do to be successful, ensuring your team supports you in your efforts for success, and making sure that your efforts are aligned with the company you are working with helps move your success forward. In a world that is in constant change, making efforts to improve yourself and move forward puts you at a competitive advantage against your peers who are staying the same. You can organize yourself to make this happen, or work with an executive coach to keep you focused on your goals. No matter what approach you take, making the effort to succeed will put you on the road to continued success.

CHAPTER EIGHT

Relationship Management for The CFO

THERE IS ONE TALENT that a Chief Financial Officer (CFO) must have to be successful—the ability to make people feel comfortable.

The CFO should not be looked up to for his or her technical abilities, but for his or her leadership qualities. The successful CFO makes people comfortable by inspiring trust. The Chief Financial Officer does this by managing expectations while exceeding them regularly. The CFO is someone who is knowledgeable about business generally and the organization he or she works for specifically. This knowledge allows the CFO to deliver on these expectations.

Identify the most successful CFO whom you know. I am willing to bet that this CFO is excellent at managing relationships. It does not matter the type of CFO he is, the industry he works in, or his technical expertise and background. It does not matter if he started his career in an accounting firm or an investment bank. The single most common thread between all different and successful CFOs is their excellence in managing relationships.

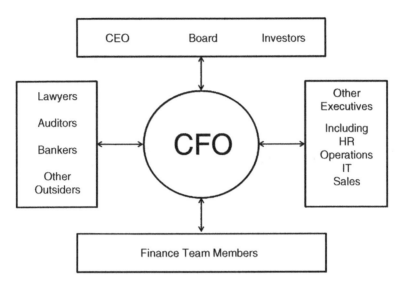

FIGURE 8.1   CFO Relationship Map

   THE CFO RELATIONSHIP MAP

Once you understand that relationships are critically important for your success as a CFO, you will want to identify the different types of relationships you will need to manage.

The CFO Relationship Map (Figure 8.1) is a visual representation of the four different types of relationships a CFO has. This map identifies you (in the middle), the people you work for (top of the map), those you work with inside your organization (right side of the map) and outside your organization (left side of the map), and the people who support you (bottom of the map).

The map includes a generalization of the people you deal with and their roles. You may deal with different people than your peer does, but all CFOs are dealing with the four groups.

Chapters 9 through 12 will discuss these specific relationships in further detail.

Are Relationships Important?

My CFO advisors think so. Ninety-six percent of my advisors believe that relationships are either important or very important to their personal success.

Their response to this question is not surprising. What is surprising to me is that they do not give this important area enough emphasis. For senior finance professionals, when the going gets tough, the tough open Excel. While senior finance executives will agree that relationships are important, I emphasize the importance of relationships to these CFOs and future CFOs because this is where the senior finance executives can have the biggest impact on their success.

What Does Your Relationship Map Look Like?

I recommend that you create your own relationship map and put it in a place where you will see regularly. This map will remind you of the importance of these relationships, who you need to positively impact, and most importantly, who you should not be forgetting.

As an executive recruiter, I have my own relationship map. My clients are on the top of the map—I am ultimately responsible to them. On the right of my map, I have candidates whom I build relationships with, and on the left, I maintain relationships with referrals. Below me, I have the team at Stanton Chase International supporting me so I can deliver on the other three relationships.

What I find interesting about my map is that the people on the top and sides move around over a period of time. For example, today's candidate can become tomorrow's client. Your relationships do not stay in one place over time, either. Keep this in mind as you manage your relationships.

Your relationship map will certainly have people you work for, people whom you work with internally and externally, as well as people who work to support you. Go ahead and map out your relationships. Be aware of your relationships, work on them, and success will surely follow.

 ## ELEMENTS OF RELATIONSHIP MANAGEMENT

I have pointed out that relationships are important and that they need to be managed. I will be discussing in the coming chapters how to manage the specifics and challenges that each of the four groups presents, as well as how to get the best out of them and overcome obstacles. Before getting into those details, we should identify what relationship management means.

What I am about to say about relationship management is common sense. This should make it easy to remember as you work to get the best out of your CFO relationships.

Knowledge

The first element in managing your relationships is knowledge. Without knowledge, the next elements cannot take place.

Be Known

People need to know who you are. Your role as CFO requires you to be visible. While you may say, "Of course, people need to know me," it is important to make yourself known. Staying in your office all day does not let people get to know you. You need to take active steps to make yourself known to the people you need to deal with.

Know Who You Are

You need to know who you are in these relationships. Relationships can only be successful when you understand your role in the relationship. If you don't know what role you play, you are at a distinct disadvantage in the relationship. Too many people assume they know who they are in the relationship. Understanding your role and confirming it for each relationship ensures you can start out right.

Know What You Can Do

When you are aware of what you (and the team that supports you) can do, you will be able to make commitments that you can deliver on. When you do not know the abilities of yourself and your team, you may miss opportunities to make a difference in your relationships. Truly knowing what you are capable of is important for relationship management.

Know Who You Need to Know

There could be many people whom you work for, who work with you, and who work for you. It may be difficult to truly know each of these people. Knowing which people you need to know, as well as the priority you need to give them, will help you manage and prioritize your relationships.

Know How to Get Your Attention

The people you work for and with, as well as those who work for you, need to know how to get your attention. It is important for your relationships that people know how to get your attention when they need you, and that you know how to prioritize the kind of attention they need. Does your CEO know how to get your attention in a business priority situation? Does your team know how to ask a low-priority question to ensure that you respond in a time-appropriate manner? Establishing these ground rules is vital to managing your relationships.

Likability

Likability builds on knowledge. Just because someone knows you doesn't mean that he likes you. Effective relationships are built on likability.

How do you get others to like you? First, you must start by liking them. The human body is a communication machine that gives off signals. If you do not like someone, that person will know. In turn, he will not like you. You do not need to say anything, because your body language will give it away.

In my role as executive recruiter and coach, I need to be able to assess people's body language for subtle clues. Learn about body language to learn about what clues you communicate so you can communicate better. Also learn about people's mannerisms so that you can understand what others are telling you with their bodies.

Second, you need to invest. Liking others is a good start to getting others to like you, but you need to invest your time, energy, and resources to get results. Your investment needs to be individualized for each person you want to build a relationship with. Without an investment, your ability to build a relationship is limited.

Trust

Once people know you and like you, they need to be able to trust you. Trust can come only when people know you and like you. Trust develops over time and can be lost in an instant. Trust is not a *yes* or *no*. There is a scale of trust, and you have to continue building trust to maintain and increase the level of trust others have in you. Trust is reciprocal. If you trust, you can gain trust. If you do not trust, you will not be trusted.

Think about a manager you once worked for who never trusted you to do the right thing. She oversaw your work like a hawk, and you always had to get permission from her to do something. Did she trust you? No. But did you trust her? Not likely. Why did you not trust her? Because you knew that she did not trust you.

Expectations

Managing expectations is the key to ongoing likeability and trust. Managing expectations requires you to have clarity on what is expected from you and delivering on those expectations. Your stretch goal should be to exceed the expectations set, but at a minimum you need to meet the expectations.

When the expectation is not a priority, not delivering on your promise may have a minor impact on you. Remember that trust is built on a scale. Minor nondelivery on expectations can reduce the scale of trust.

When you do not provide an important deliverable as expected, your actions (or inactions) can have a disastrous effect on your relationships. Unlike when you miss delivery on minor expectations, major expectation gaffes have the ability to instantly reduce your trust factor to zero. Missing important expectations can lead to a reduction in your likability, as well.

When likability and trust disappear from your relationships, you need to be aware that your time at your current employer may be coming to a close.

 EXAMPLES OF SUCCESSFUL CFO RELATIONSHIP MANAGEMENT

It is easy to talk theory about how relationships have a positive impact on the success of a CFO. For practical examples, I asked my CFO advisors to discuss how their relationships improved their success at their employers. Here are some of their interesting personal experiences:

> I developed a structured communication process. This included weekly meetings for the entire executive team, and weekly one-on-one meetings with the CEO, Chief Operating Officer, and Vice President Sales. I also instituted a two-way open door policy with CEO.
>
> I am a partner in addition to being the CFO. Strong trust and credibility has been developed among all partners of the firm and is crucial for our success. In a recent share valuation conflict, it was critical that all partners were open to receiving

the facts and openly discussing the details before proceeding objectively and fairly. Without the leverage of trust between us, this emotionally charged issue could not have been resolved in a fair and balanced way. It would have required bringing in outside expertise to mediate. I mediated the successful conclusion of this conflict.

I maintained a good working relationship with our banker, who left one bank to go to another. I was able to switch banks and secure almost a 50 percent reduction in our average debt interest rates.

Everything I do is about influence at the executive level. I quite often find it's important to understand who else I might need to have support something I'm ultimately conveying to the CEO and different functions will have sway, depending on what's being discussed or considered. A good example has been around our international expansion where we are frequently considering locations and entities before our need. However, that has financial and other repercussions, so I've been trying to slow it down and have it be a more considered step in the overall process.

I was hired as CFO for a fabulously successful company where the primary owner believed cash was king and the finance department was run by command and control, not customer service. By building a relationship with them I was able to transform the department to a value-added customer-service-driven department. This increased the overall value provided to the company and the stakeholders.

Some of the most rewarding relationships have been with the sales side of the business when working together to structure transactions. It clearly allowed our company to get new business, while managing risks in an effective way to achieve the corporate goals.

I became the face of the company with all our major suppliers and was able to negotiate better terms and implement highly effective lean initiatives with these suppliers. This made the company significantly more effective at meeting customer needs and led to a measurable increase in market share. These types of relationships could only be established through a high-level person such as the CFO.

These examples should give you an appreciation of what happens when the CFO makes the effort to build relationships and their potential impact.

EXAMPLES OF FAILED CFO RELATIONSHIPS

Not all relationships work. Our previous stories of successful CFO relationships need to be counterbalanced by insights into relationships that did not work. Here are some anecdotes provided by my CFO advisors:

> I did not educate my prior CEO on my role and expectations. He had not worked before (anywhere) and didn't understand much of what a CFO does. It wasn't a satisfying relationship for either of us.

> There was no structure to communications and no one-on-one discussions, either. I avoided the CEO because I thought he wanted to make all the decisions. He thought I was doing well and I would come to him if I needed help. Neither of us engaged with each other. This was not a recipe for success.

> At a former company, the CEO did not value the role of a CFO as he never had worked with one in the past. As a result, the more I tried to engage and work with him, the more he pushed me off to the COO. This limited my ability to lead my team, have the impact I desired, and be included in the decision-making DNA of the company. I eventually left as I was frustrated with the diminished role and lack of involvement with key decisions.

> We did not prepare our bank for potential covenant violations. This led to tense negotiations that wasted time and had a negative impact on our business.

> Information technology costs were spiraling out of control. This resulted in friction between me and the CIO. It did not get resolved early enough as we did not see beyond our points of view, which resulted in mistrust. Later on both of us decided to get an independent review done and we were able to find common ground.

> At a former organization, the CEO was not open and honest in his communications and would berate staff for speaking up. It was a hostile environment for making change or suggesting improvements. Many good people would no longer participate at meetings and most of us ultimately left.

> Conflict avoidance, and "hope as a strategy" never works out well. Not addressing key issues head on, in an open and collaborative environment, only fosters negative perceptions, and perception, to most, is reality. Improper management of perceptions and expectations is a CFO killer.

I had a CEO who wanted a yes-man and could not understand that when we looked at the same situation we had different perspectives and the combination of both perspectives provided balance as opposed to emphasizing the differences. This really helped me realize the nature of the position I would thrive best in, which is where I could be part of a collaborative open dialogue as opposed to one opinion only being considered. In this particular case we butted heads constantly and ultimately I left. He hired two people to replace me to do his bidding.

I worked at one company where bankers were not communicated with frequently. As a result, when funding was needed they were unwilling to stretch their limits. This required us to look beyond traditional financing and ultimately resulted in an acquisition not being able to close.

 ## WHY DO CFO RELATIONSHIPS FAIL?

The situations described by my CFO advisors are examples of failed relationships that had a negative impact on the CFO.

When people think of the word *relationship*, they tend to apply it to the personal, romantic type of relationship. In a business context, relationships are more similar to parent, sibling, and extended family relationships than personal, romantic relationships. As CFO, your relationships are more than a number of individual, personal, one-on-one interactions. Your map may look linear, but in reality you are living in a relationship *matrix*.

We see that relationships in a business environment can be complicated. When relationships fail, can they be fixed? The answer is, some can be fixed, some cannot.

Before seeing if we can fix a relationship, let us identify the reasons that relationships fail.

Inherent or Systemic Issues

In one of the previous examples, the CFO said that his CEO was not open and honest, and that the CEO fostered a hostile environment. This is one example of an instance where key people (individually or collectively) are an important factor in creating the right environment for relationship failure.

Lack of Effort

When sufficient effort has not been put into a relationship, challenges arise that may cause disappointment. In one example of failure mentioned in the previous section, the bank was not willing to go the extra mile when the company needed help, because there was no effort invested in an ongoing and open relationship with the bank.

Lack of Common Ground

In another example, the CFO had difficulty with the CIO in working together managing IT costs. In this case, the CFO was focused on cost containment, and the CIO was motivated to meet the business challenges with the most appropriate technology. When two people in a relationship are not on the same page, it is a challenge for them to find common ground to solve conflicts that arise.

Lack of Trust

Just because you have to work with someone as CFO, it does not mean that you trust each other. You cannot be successful in your relationship with another person without a decent level of trust. In another of the examples provided by my CFO advisors, the CEO did not work with the CFO and passed off the relationship to the Chief Operating Officer. It is hard to know why they CEO did this, but if the CEO had trusted the CFO, the CEO would not have passed the relationship off to the COO in the first place.

Having identified the different reasons for failed relationships, let's discuss if these failures can be corrected.

Know What Cannot Change

When a CFO comes to the realization that a relationship cannot change and improve, there is only one of two solutions: You go, or the other individual goes. Many CFOs I have spoken with tell me that they left their positions because they no longer wanted to be in a situation where they could not make the changes needed for their success. It can happen in some cases that the party who cannot change will leave (or be asked to leave). This can happen to the CEO, your executive peers, your outside relationships, and your team.

Know What Can Change

Leaving a difficult relationship (quitting) can be easier than repeatedly trying to make it work. Before leaving a difficult relationship, it is important to identify areas of common ground to see whether the relationship can be improved. Not every challenge in your relationships with others can be overcome, but it is your responsibility as Chief Financial Officer to try. Your experience can help you understand what to do in difficult situations and know whom to turn to in order to accomplish your goals. When you find common ground to agree upon, you have the opportunity to build from there. If you know what can change and come up with an approach to effect that change, you are doing your part to make a difference.

CONCLUSION

- We identified the importance of relationships to a CFO's success.
- We mapped the different types of CFO relationships.
- We discussed the value of mapping your own relationships.
- We spoke about the four elements needed for building and maintaining successful relationships.
- We reviewed actual situations of successful and failed CFO relationships.
- We explained why CFO relationships fail, and what, if anything, can be done to correct them.

The common factor between successful CFOs, no matter their background or experience, is their ability to maintain and nurture excellent relationships. As CFO, you need to know whom you interact with, and the CFO Relationship Map can be a useful tool in visualizing this. Successful relationships can only exist when there is knowledge, esteem, and trust between the individuals and the expectations between them are managed properly. When a CFO learns from her relationship successes and failures in the past and builds on them, she can get the best out of them and continue to succeed and thrive.

CHAPTER NINE

Relationships with the CEO, Board, and Investors

I N CHAPTER 8 WE introduced the CFO Relationship Map (see Figure 8.1). The map is a representation of the relationships a CFO has. This chapter deals with the relationships CFOs have with the people they work for, including the CEO, the Board of Directors of the company, as well as the company's investors (or owners).

 ## THE CEO RELATIONSHIP

The CEO is the person whom the CFO most often reports to, but there can be exceptions. In some circumstances, the CFO could report to someone who reports to the CEO. This person would usually have the title of Chief Operating Officer or President. The CEO may or may not sit on the Board of Directors. When sitting on the board, the CEO may also be the Chairman of the Board, as well. In some companies, the CEO is not only the person in charge of the management of the company; he may own a significant portion of the company, as well.

In essence, the CEO role scales from one end where the individual has solely a management role, to the other end where the CEO is the chief manager of the business as well as the owner. The latter case is more likely in an owner-managed business, which tends to be smaller in size and scope than a business with a professional manager in the CEO role.

This chapter discusses the CFO's relationship with a CEO, board, and investors in a situation where the roles are separate and distinct. This may not exactly describe your current situation, specifically if you work in an owner-managed business. However, the examples and discussion that follow do apply to the different roles that the owner-manager fills. (We will identify areas at the end of this chapter that apply differently to an owner-managed business.)

CFOs at larger corporate entities may report to a business unit CEO but not be directly responsible to a Board of Directors or investors. The business unit CFO in many cases reports to the corporate CFO in addition to the business unit CEO. In such a case, the corporate CFO can be considered to have a board-like impact on the business unit CFO. (At the end of the chapter, we identify specifics that need to be considered for a business unit CFO.)

Keys to a Successful CEO Relationship

The following sections provide some keys to a successful relationship with your CEO.

Each CEO Is Unique

You are not like all the other CFOs. Your CEO is not like all the other CEOs, either. Each CEO is a unique individual with her own skills, experiences, and knowledge that she brings to the table, combined with an individualized style that makes her who she is.

It is important that you understand your CEO well. Know her background and understand what she brings to the table. Be aware of how she acts with you and interacts with others. Understand what makes her happy and makes her tick. Recognize what her body language is telling you. The better you are at reading and anticipating your CEO, the more productive and effective you will be.

Support Your CEO

A successful relationship with your CEO requires that he knows that you are there to support him. You have your responsibilities to oversee and manage the financial aspects of the business, but your CEO needs to know (and be reminded) that you are there to help him succeed.

Thack Brown was CFO–Latin America at SAP from 2008 to 2013, and is now the Chief Operating Officer–Latin America at SAP. Brown recommends that CFOs sit and spend time in the office of the CEO and say, "What are we working on? What are the strategic challenges that we need to go after? What help do you need?" Brown believes that the CEO is waiting for you to do this, and will be grateful when you approach him.

Just as your finance team is critical to your success, you play a very important role in your CEO's success. Ensuring that you are there and available to support him is important. Take the time to understand your CEO's needs. Discuss the business challenges he is facing. Provide him with the numerical support to make business decisions as well as the personal support to stand by him.

Obviously, communication is key to be able to support your CEO. Build a relationship that allows for regular, scheduled one-on-one meetings with your CEO. Work with your CEO to develop an open-door policy that works both ways. Build a relationship that fosters mutual trust. Your CEO needs you to be a partner in his or her success.

Number Two

In addition to supporting the CEO, many CFOs are considered second in command. In a good number of companies, the CFO is looked at as the person who has the CEO's ear and serves as his or her right-hand person.

This positioning as second in command does not happen by itself. As CFO, how you interact with your CEO and how others see you doing so can build the perception that you are the confidant of the CEO. When your CEO mentions to people inside and outside the company that she needs to get the CFO's input before making major decisions, you will know you have achieved number-two status.

Your CEO needs guidance, counsel, and support in moving the corporate objectives forward. The more you provide him or her with this backing, the more he or she will rely on you and the more successful you will be in your CFO role.

Trust

Trust is important to any relationship. For the CEO/CFO relationship, trust is the glue that makes the twosome an effective team. In Chapter 8, trust was mentioned as a key element for successful relationship management. At the risk of generalizing, a good number of finance executives have a tendency to be skeptical and conservative, while many CEOs tend to have a more speculative nature, with a propensity for selling the positive aspects while minimizing the negatives. These inherent differences between the CFO and CEO can make trust challenging.

For the CFO, having the CEO trust you is absolutely critical for you to be successful. When the CEO trusts you to be his right hand and seeks out your input, guidance, and insight, you are able to accomplish and succeed in your CFO role.

As CFO you also need to be able to trust your CEO. The conservative nature of a typical CFO can clash with the speculative nature of a typical CEO. This can make it difficult for the CFO to completely trust the CEO. If you cannot trust your CEO, you cannot perform your CFO duties with confidence.

From my experiences talking with CFOs over the years, the biggest challenge faced by CFOs is a lack of trust between the CEO and CFO. When trust begins to falter in this relationship, it is only a matter of time before the CFO is no longer with the company.

Respect

With trust, comes respect. In the optimal CEO/CFO relationship, mutual respect reigns. When respect is not a strong part of this relationship, the CFO's ability to deliver is weakened.

When CFOs trust their CEOs, they have the confidence to act appropriately and deliver to the best of their abilities. When CEOs trust their CFOs, they can spend less time second guessing the CFO and focus on ensuring the company is meeting its overall objectives and strategies.

Priorities

Managing priorities is a constant challenge for the CFO. There are many things that need to get done and only so much time to get them done in. CFOs not only need to manage and prioritize their direct responsibilities; it is critical that they ensure that the CEOs' priorities are taken care of, as well.

The only way a CFO will know what the CEO's priorities are is by keeping an open channel for communication. Giving priority to what is important to the CEO will assist you in strengthening your relationship with him or her.

Communication

Assume nothing. Get clarity on what you need to get done and what is expected of you. You must know what the CEO is thinking. You can only deliver to the CEO if you know what he needs and expects from you.

The ideal situation for a CFO is when the CEO wants and needs to hear what you think, even if you disagree with her. This can happen only if you understand how your CEO thinks, acts, and reacts. You need to know how she likes to hear good news, and more importantly, the best way to break bad news to her.

Listening is a critical skill when dealing with your CEO. Knowing how to listen to your boss is very important. Does he want your feedback immediately? Does he simply want the opportunity to vent his frustrations? Does he want you to come up with a solution to the challenge being addressed?

The successful CFO has excellent communication skills and continually works on improving them. Having a strong and positive relationship with your CEO requires your attention, awareness, and continuous improvement of any and all issues regarding communicating with your CEO.

Goal Setting

Chapter 7 identified the importance of setting goals for yourself and your finance team. As CFO, you work for and report to the CEO. The goals you set out to accomplish require input from your CEO. Knowing what this individual wants and needs you to accomplish, as well as regular communication about the status of attaining these objectives, is an important part of your relationship with your CEO.

Setting these goals should be a collaborative process. Not only do you need to know what the CEO wants you to achieve, but you need to have a vision of the reality you would like to have a positive impact on. Formulating your objectives based on the knowledge, experience, and abilities of yourself and the team that supports you allows the CEO to have confidence in your abilities and your understanding of what is important for the company to succeed.

Strategy

As CFO, strategic direction of the business is not your primary responsibility. However, your input in creating and changing strategy is of utmost importance. You are the official scorekeeper, knower of profit and loss. The ideas for the big picture of the future of the business may come from those in the trenches (the operational executives) and the General leading them (the CEO), but you are the interpreter of business action into business dollars. Your understanding of the business, how it works, and how it translates into monetary success is what you bring to the table.

As the CEO leads strategic development to long-term planning and short-term issues, your translation and hole-poking skills are necessary to ensure that the dream can become a profitable reality.

Resources

Your ability to deliver value to the CEO is dependent on the resources available to you. In Chapter 1, I noted that more than three-quarters of my CFO advisors feel they put in more than 110 percent effort into their roles as CFOs. When CFOs put so much effort into their jobs, it is important that they have the resources necessary to meet the demands of their roles and the needs of their CEOs.

We have mentioned numerous times in this book that CFOs can only be as good as their teams allow them to be. We will discuss issues related to building and developing the best finance team for your needs in Chapter 12. In the meantime, as it relates to your relationship with the CEO, you need to ensure that you have the proper resources available to you to properly do your job and meet the CEO's needs. It is important to make the CEO aware of resource challenges you face in being able to deliver on your mutually agreed-upon goals.

It is important to mention at this time that CFOs often find themselves between a rock and a hard place when it comes to resources. With CFOs having the responsibility of ensuring financial accountability, they spend a good part of their effort keeping different parts of the business under financial control. When CFOs are asking others in the company to do more with less, it is morally challenging for them to increase their spending on resources.

In Chapter 10, we will discuss more about working with your fellow executives. In the meantime, it is important to note that you have a responsibility to get the resources you to need to deliver. You need to make the case to the CEO that your challenges are important and that he can have confidence giving you the financial, human, and technical resources you need to support the company in meeting its objectives. If you truly believe that you need more to accomplish more, make your case. Be mindful that you have to be careful about company resources, but don't use this as an excuse to have a lean team that is not able to deliver what it—and you—must.

How Strong Is Your CEO Relationship?

Rate the strength of your CEO relationship:

Very weak   _____
Weak   _____
Neither   _____
Strong   _____
Very strong   _____

How much room for improvement do you have in your relationship with your CEO?

A lot   _____
A little   _____
It's good, but could be better   _____
It couldn't be better   _____

Areas for improvement

1. _____
2. _____
3. _____

Detail your plan for improving your relationship with your CEO:

_____
_____
_____

RELATIONSHIP WITH YOUR BOARD OF DIRECTORS

The Board of Directors is the governance body appointed by the shareholders of the company to oversee the management of the company. Ultimately answering to the shareholders, board members have a fiduciary responsibility to act in the company's best interests. As the financial leader in your company, you have an important impact on the Board of Directors in providing them with information so they can properly meet their responsibilities. The Board of Directors needs a strong, capable, and ethical CFO to do its job.

Not all companies have an active Board of Directors. In businesses that are owner-managed, most, if not all, of their directors are actively involved in the business. Family-held businesses have their own dynamics, which we will address toward the end of the chapter. Companies that have outside investors generally have an active Board of Directors that provides oversight to management. This section deals with companies that have an active board.

It is essential for CFOs to know what their board requires from them so they can meet these needs. An excellent reference document is "Financial Aspects of Governance: What Boards Should Expect from CFOs," written by Hugh Lindsay and published by the Canadian Institute of Chartered Accountants (http://www.cica.ca/focus-on-practice-areas/governance-strategy-and-risk/cfo-series/item12316.pdf). Knowing what boards expect from you will allow you to deliver what they need. This quote from the document explains how a CFO can help the board.

> *The CFO is a valuable resource to boards as the internal expert who can present important financial information to the directors in a credible, relevant and understandable way. CFOs should attend Board meetings and be prepared to meet directors' needs for information, explanations and clarification both in structured presentations and in response to questions. They can also help Board members by providing additional reference material.*

Having a strong and effective relationship with your board is critical to your success. Understanding what board members need and delivering to their expectations is a critical component of your success.

Who Is the Boss?

One of the biggest challenges facing CFOs is knowing who they really are responsible to. Is the CFO responsible to the CEO or to the board? Does it have to be one or the other, or can it be both? If CFOs are really responsible to both, how should they manage that dual responsibility?

In one way, this dual responsibility is like any other relationship you've had with someone you have reported to earlier in your career. You may have had a superior, but that individual had a boss, too. Your ongoing responsibility was to your direct supervisor, but you realized that you had a commitment to your boss's boss and to the company as a whole. You've done this for your entire career. Now that you're a CFO, is it really that different?

It can be different. Many boards have expectations that the CFO is another set of eyes and ears for them in delivering their fiduciary responsibility to the company. Some board members may want to hear things directly from you without filtering by the CEO. What is the best way to manage these multiple reporting relationships?

When placing CFOs with new companies, I always recommend that they spend the time upfront to understand what is expected of them by the Board of Directors. Before accepting a role with a new company, the CFO candidate should at least have a conversation with the Chairman of the Board, the audit committee chairman, or both of them. Knowing what the board expects from you before accepting a new CFO position is an important part of ensuring an ongoing optimal relationship with the board.

CFOs should never forget that the board can fire the CEO.

Not One Relationship, but Many

Your Board of Directors is composed of a number of people. You do not have one relationship with the board but relationships with many people. Certainly, you will not have the same relationship with each board member. Some board relationships will be strong and ongoing while others will be sporadic.

It is important that you know the board members. Understanding their backgrounds, strengths, and biases will allow you to modify your personal interaction with them in the best way possible.

Background

Where are they coming from? What can you learn from them? What individual perspectives are they bringing to the table that you and your company can benefit from? Did they experience issues at another company that were similar to what your company is currently facing? Were any of them in a CFO role before? Are they important and high-profile people, who nevertheless cannot understand your industry, company, or specific situation well enough to provide value to you and the company?

Strengths

What are the strengths of each of your company's board members? Do their strengths complement one another? How can you take best advantage of those strengths? How can you support those strengths with yours? What strengths do you have that can support key board members in accomplishing their objectives? Are there any key strengths missing from the board, and if so, what can you do to help?

Biases

Each individual board member comes to the table with his or her own agenda. These biases may be difficult to assess, but usually they are based on who the directors are representing. A truly independent board member will have the interest of all shareholders in mind. The board member representing a specific shareholder, such as the majority shareholder or a certain group of investors, will have those interests top of mind. The founder and his or her representative will be looking out for their best interests, while private equity or venture capital investors will be looking at their investment timeline and potential return as a priority. Knowing who ultimately wants what from their positions on the board is critical to understanding board dynamics and your impact on them.

I have heard stories from CFOs of soap opera–like challenges in the boardroom. This may not happen in your company, yet you need to be aware of the agendas of the people you ultimately report to. Trying to keep everyone happy runs the risk of making no one happy.

Expectation Management

Managing expectations was noted as one of the key elements of relationship success (Chapter 8). Managing the expectations of your Board of Directors is critical to ensuring your continued success with your company.

No Surprises

Board members are generally not involved in the day-to-day operations and issues of your business. Considering that they have the ultimate fiduciary responsibility for the company, they need to know all important news—the good and the bad. It may be acceptable to share good news as a surprise, but it is never good to share bad news as a surprise. Waiting until a board meeting to share information about a catastrophic loss has the potential to be a serious career-limiting move. Never sideswipe a board.

Deliver What They Want

In your meetings with your board members, be sure you hear what they are asking you for. If they want a report on an ongoing situation, make sure you update them as requested. If a board member wants information at the board meeting but the information is not available during the meeting, ensure that you get this information to the board member as soon as possible afterward. If you are not certain about what they were seeking from you, confirm it during the meeting or, if that is not possible, as soon as possible thereafter. When confirming what they want, make sure you know when they expect the response. Any request from a board member is a high-priority request unless you are told otherwise. Not delivering what has been asked for can put a significant tarnish on your shine that may be difficult to overcome.

Presentation Matters

Do not treat meetings with the board like you would meetings with your team. "Back of the napkin" is not acceptable. How you present your information shows how important you consider them. Your board has limited time. The members want to see information, not data. The information must be well presented in a format that is well summarized, clear, and crisp. Your presentation should provide the appropriate and relevant information to get your key points across. Find a balance between providing too much information and not leaving important details out. Be prepared with backup answers and materials to make a point if clarity is needed. You cannot wing a board meeting.

Uncover the Unmentioned Expectations

Meeting expectations is challenging enough when you know what is expected from you. When dealing with a group as diverse and experienced as a Board of Directors, you need to find out what they really expect from you. This exercise is not a one-time conversation but an ongoing challenge that requires that you combine the political skills you have learned over your career with your ability to "read the tea leaves." The closer the relationships you build with board members, the more they will be willing to share with you about their expectations as well as what they believe their colleagues expect from you. Know the score; understand how your board keeps it.

Key Board Relationships

Each board member is important. Some are more important for the CFO. Below, I have identified the key board members that are important for you to interact with, and some items you should keep in mind as you work with them.

Chairman

The Chairman is the leader of the board, and, depending on the specific bylaws governing your company, can have various responsibilities. Generally, the

Chairman guides the board, chairs the board meetings, and acts as the representative and spokesperson of the board.

The Chairman is an important person with whom to have a positive relationship. As your superior's ultimate boss, developing a positive relationship with this individual is critical to your success at the company. Building affinity and trust with the Chairman, as well as managing, meeting, and exceeding expectations, is crucial.

However, when the Chairman and the CEO are the same person, your relationship concerns are the same as mentioned in the previous section, "The CEO Relationship."

Founder

In some companies, the person who founded the company remains a shareholder. The founder may no longer be involved in the day-to-day operations of the business, but remains active on the board in some capacity.

Building a relationship with the founder (or founders) is important because they really know the business. They have lived through the culture and challenges from the beginning and have an institutional knowledge that can be very helpful to the CFO in carrying out his duties. It can also be worthwhile for the CFO to have the founder as an admirer and supporter. In key issues and challenges that can arise at the board table, having the founder on your side can be valuable.

Audit Committee

A significant portion of a CFO's interaction with her board will be with this committee. The *audit committee* is an active group of board members who involve themselves with the supervision of financial reporting. This committee should exist in all publicly listed companies and can exist in companies where there are outside investors. As the person responsible for the financial management of the company, the CFO will be directly involved with this committee.

Financial reporting and internal control issues have been given more prominence since the beginning of the century due to regulatory matters such as the Sarbanes-Oxley and Dodd-Frank acts in the United States (and similar regulations that have followed in other countries).

The audit committee chairman is the most important person on the board for the CFO to develop a positive relationship with. Understanding the concerns of the chair and the committee, addressing them in a timely manner, and working with them to secure the support and resources necessary to ensure proper financial management and reporting are critical areas in which the CFO needs to be successful.

CFOs with a strong financial reporting and internal control background are at an advantage when dealing with the audit committee. These CFOs can be directly involved with ensuring that these issues are dealt with properly and on a timely basis. In companies where the CFO does not have sufficient financial reporting experience, she will have to rely upon her most senior team leaders responsible for this area. Regardless whether the CFO is the "GAAP king" or relies on his team for this responsibility, appropriate and successful interaction with the audit committee is key to the CFO's success with the board.

Challenges at the audit committee level can be detrimental to the success and tenure of any CFO. This relationship needs an investment of time and resources to ensure success.

The audit committee relationship with the CFO becomes more difficult when you add the external auditor to the mix. We will discuss the CFO's relationship with the external auditor in Chapter 11, Relationships with Outsiders.

Compensation Committee

Before explaining the need for the involvement of the CFO with the compensation committee, it is important to understand the role of this committee. According to the Deloitte Center for Corporate Governance website (www .corpgov.deloitte.com/site/us/compensation-committee/):

> *The role of the compensation committee is to set appropriate and supportable pay programs that are in the organization's best interests and aligned with its business mission and strategy.*

In reading this explanation about the role of the compensation committee, my first thought was, this is a human resources issue, not a financial issue, and it should be dealt with by the senior executive in charge of human resources, not finance. Yet upon reflection, it is clear there are issues where the CFO needs to be involved.

Reporting of Benefits, Including Options

There is a financial reporting impact of benefits given to employees and executives of the company. The involvement of finance in the creation and modification of these programs is necessary and helpful.

Financial Impact

Human Resources is responsible for the human capital issues in a company while Finance is responsible for the financial issues. In most companies, the cost of human capital is a significant component of total company costs. As a key leader responsible for the financial well-being of the company, your involvement as CFO is necessary to ensure the financial ramifications are taken into consideration when developing and setting compensation policies.

Executive Compensation

In many companies, the CFO is the most visible executive at the board table other than the CEO. (Exceptions can include when a company has a COO, President, or General Counsel.) Your performance at the board table will be noted and will have an impact on what you earn when executive compensation is reviewed. Winning friends and influencing people at the board table can have an indirect positive impact on your personal income.

The CEO Roadblock

There are different types of CEOs. When a Chief Executive Officer has issues with control and trust, the relationship between a CFO and the board can be stymied and challenged.

In my career in executive search, I have spoken with CFOs who have confided in me that they have faced this type of CEO. These CFOs told me that they were not allowed to present to the board or even speak with any board member in an official or unofficial capacity without going through the CEO. I remember one CFO telling me that this situation prevented him from building a relationship of trust with the board. The CFO said that when the company was facing some serious challenges, he was not able to reach out and have a discussion that could help the company overcome these problems.

In many cases, a powerful CEO not only dominates and controls management, but does the same thing to the board, as well. When a board finds itself in a situation where its members cannot develop relationships with key executives without the oversight of the CEO, it should be wary that it could find itself in a situation where it is not able to properly deliver on its fiduciary responsibilities.

CFOs should question whether remaining in such an atmosphere will allow them to succeed. Few work environments are perfect, but being limited in such a manner may not allow CFOs to deliver on their responsibilities.

Board Disagreements

Anyone who follows corporate news in the United States knows that board disagreements have the ability to make news. In August 2013, a J.C. Penney board member resigned "as a result of a disagreement with decisions made by the board of directors and the timing and process surrounding the CEO search" (www.sec.gov/Archives/edgar/data/1166126/000116612613000055/ jcpenney8kaug1213.htm).

For every board dispute that ends up in the press, there are many more that go unpublicized. Disagreements of all sizes happen often at the board table. Sometimes they end up in the news. Most times they end up consuming time, effort, and energy.

As CFO, you will be pulled into such disputes. Some of these disputes, if you're lucky, are about strategy and ways to move forward. In these cases, your involvement may not be significant. However, many disputes have a financial component to them, and, as the person with access to the company's financial information, you will be called on to provide information. You might even be called upon by your CEO to pick a side in the disagreement.

Try to stay as neutral as possible in these disputes. The only reasons you might consider picking a side in a board dispute include:

- There is a clear moral case between right and wrong.
- The winner in the dispute is clear and you choose the winning side.
- Your incentives for backing one side of the disagreement over the other have a very positive impact on your career and income.
- Not choosing a side will only put you in a losing proposition (i.e., you are forced to choose a side).

Whatever situation you face, be aware that board disputes can be a minefield for a CFO. Tread with caution.

Providing Value

We have covered a number of topics in the area of the CFO's relationship with the Board of Directors. While we did not cover the entire gamut of possible issues and concerns when it comes to your relations with the board, I covered some key areas that I have seen CFOs needing to deal with.

The overriding factor when it comes to CFOs having successful relationships with their board members is to keep these two words in mind: *Provide value*. No matter what your board looks like or how its members interact with you, your goal is to continue to provide value to the board. Keep doing this and you will develop successful, long-term board relationships.

How Strong Are Your Board Relationships?

Rate the strength of your board relationships:

Very weak   _____
Weak   _____
Neither   _____
Strong   _____
Very strong   _____

How much room for improvement do you have in your board relationships?

A lot   _____
A little   _____
They are good, but could be better   _____
They could not be better   _____

Who are the key people on the board whom you need to have an excellent relationship with?

1. _____
2. _____
3. _____

Areas for improvement:

1. _____
2. _____
3. _____

Detail your plan for improving your board relationships:

_____
_____
_____

RELATIONSHIP WITH INVESTORS

The CFO Relationship Map puts the investor at the top together with the CEO and the Board of Directors. The CFO certainly works for the CEO and does work for and report to the board, but does the CFO really work for the investor?

In preparing the relationship map, I could have considered putting the topic of relations with investors on the left side of the map in the area depicting people you deal with outside your organization. In some ways, dealing with investors is similar to dealing with lenders, as both provide funding to the company.

Lenders provide debt financing and have a contractual relationship with the company. The CFO does not work for the lender. (We will discuss the CFO's relationship with bankers in Chapter 11.)

Shareholders, however, appoint the Board of Directors to represent their interests in the oversight and control of the company. The Board of Directors hires management to run the company. From a contractual point of view, the CFO is not an employee of the investor, but an employee of the company owned by the shareholders. Ultimately, the CFO does have a responsibility to the owners of the company. In the end, the Chief Financial Officer does work for the shareholder.

To learn more about investor relations (IR), I spoke with David Calusdian, Executive Vice President and Partner at Sharon Merrill, an investor relations and crisis communications firm based in Boston, working with companies across the United States.

Importance of Investor Relations

Calusdian says the primary reason CFOs need to effectively connect with shareholders is to develop relationships with current and future investors that will ultimately impact the company's cost of capital.

> **Note:** This section discusses relationships with investors who are not actively involved in the company. Where the shareholders are actively involved in the business, this section is not relevant. For a further discussion on the issues of managing relationships in owner-managed or closely held businesses, read the relevant section at the end of this chapter.

His point about developing relationships with current and future investors should resonate with CFOs. As Chief Financial Officer, you want to ensure that your current investors stay invested in your company and consider making further investments in your company. When the CFO takes the responsibility of investor relations seriously, a good amount of time devoted to this area will be focused on building relationships with future investors, as well.

CFOs are responsible for ensuring that they have the funds they need when they need them so the company can accomplish its goals. While this book is not intended to give economics or finance lessons, people with finance experience should understand that the more people want to invest in your company, the easier and cheaper it will be for the CFO to access sources of funding.

Who Is Responsible for Investor Relations?

The CEO is the usually the ultimate spokesperson for any company. In this capacity, some CEOs are directly involved in the investor relations role, both in terms of keeping current shareholders happy and developing new investors. When the CEO is front and center in this capacity, the CFO takes an important support role for the CEO.

When a company is looking to raise a new round of financing, whether it be from institutional investors or from a public offering, the CEO's involvement is required. People want to see and hear from the boss. When going on a road-show to showcase the company and its investment potential, the CEO and CFO need to work as a cohesive team.

Managing the Investor Relationship

Here is how the basics for successful relationship management (as mentioned in Chapter 8) can be applied to the investor relationship.

> **Tip:** CFOs need to be aware that road-shows can be an overwhelming time commitment that can take them away from their ongoing, normal CFO responsibilities. Planning properly to ensure that your team can take over some key tasks will allow you to focus more of your attention on this important company priority.

Knowledge

The critical first step when dealing with investors is letting them know who you are. Investors are people who are looking to place their money with a company that will meet their investment criteria. You can only be considered by investors who know about you. A key part of an investor relations strategy is to get investors to know about you. Only then can they assess whether you are an appropriate investment for them. If they don't know you, they certainly will not invest.

Sharon Merrill's Calusdian recommends that companies be proactive in their investor relations and not just reactive. This includes identifying potential new investor prospects and reaching out to them. He also recommends reaching out to investment analysts that cover your industry. He believes that too many companies miss the proactive opportunities, and this needs to be included in a company's investor relations action plan.

Likability

Once current and potential investors know about you, you want them to like you. How can an investor like a company? It's all in the story.

Your company has a story. You know the story. You bought into it as an employee. It is the tale about what makes your company unique and different. Is your company likeable because it has a compelling, life-changing product or service? Is it likeable because the company has an ability to make the investor a lot of money? Is it a combination of the two?

Calusdian's experience consulting with companies over the years has helped his clients develop their compelling stories. He feels that an area many CFOs can further develop is their ability to tell the story. "Effective presentation training and media coaching are important so that the CFO can be the best face of the company they can be," Calusdian said.

Getting investors to like your company requires a compelling story and an ability to get that story across in an effective and interesting way.

Trust

When you ask people to put their money in your company, they have to trust you. Knowing of your company is not enough and neither is liking your company's story. To invest in you and your company, people need to trust that you can deliver on the story they are interested in.

For most investors trust comes down to trusting the people running the company. Think about investment stories like Nortel and BlackBerry (formerly Research In Motion). Both of these companies were successful stocks that were considered darlings of the stock market (in their heyday). Their stories may have still been compelling, but their share prices were affected dramatically when the ability of both companies' management teams to deliver on those stories could no longer be trusted.

As mentioned in the previous chapter, trust develops over time and can be lost in an instant. Your role as the person in charge of investor relations is to provide compelling reasons for investors to continue to trust the story you tell about your company.

Expectations

Once trust is developed to the point of investors putting their money into your company, you need to continue to keep that trust by communicating what you will deliver and meeting or exceeding those expectations.

Calusdian believes that managing expectations is key for successful investor relations. "Investors buy on the future of the company and investors have expectations as to what the company will achieve, so if the company does not fulfill their expectations and disappoints them, it reflects on the stock price and the evaluation." "Underpromising and overdelivering" is a catchphrase for success in investor relations.

Calusdian also says that "the key challenge that CFOs have is to make sure that they are communicating effectively and that they are being transparent with the investment community regarding their prospects, while at the same time trying to meet or beat the street's expectations."

Communicating Bad News

Not all news is good. It is easy to share good news. How should a company disclose bad news?

Calusdian says that public companies in the United States, first and foremost, must abide by Securities and Exchange Commission (SEC) disclosure rules, including Regulation Fair Disclosure (Regulation FD). But beyond that, when communicating bad news, he believes that it is important to be transparent with investors about the problem while also explaining what the company is doing to rectify the situation.

Investor Relations for the Growth Company

Companies that are public require an *investor relations* function within the Finance group led by the CFO. What about companies that are not public but are in growth mode and need to finance that growth?

I asked Calusdian what he thinks is the right time for a growth company to start considering developing an investor relations function. He said that for companies that are not yet public but have plans to go public, acting like a public company is the best way to prepare to go public. This requires having the right infrastructure in place so that you can effectively communicate what is going on at the company on a regular basis. You want investors to be accustomed to seeing that type of information flowing from the company. Calusdian said that management should get used to communicating and evaluating what is newsworthy.

How Effective Are Your Investor Relationships?

Rate the strength of your investor relations:

Very weak   _____
Weak   _____
Neither   _____
Strong   _____
Very strong   _____

How much room for improvement do you have in your investor relationships?

A lot   _____
A little   _____
They are good, but could be better   _____
They couldn't be better   _____

Who are the key investor groups that you need to develop better relationships with?

1. _____
2. _____
3. _____

Areas for improvement:

1. _____
2. _____
3. _____

Detail your plan for improving your investor relations:

_____
_____
_____

OTHER SITUATIONS

The relationships described previously are common in many corporate circumstances, but not all. There are situations where a CFO may not work for a
CEO, may not report to a board, and may not work for investors. The discussion
so far in this chapter can provide the CFO with strategies on how to handle
different situations with similar characteristics. In the next section, I address
other situations that CFOs may face in who they report to.

Owner-Managed Business

When the CEO of the company is also the owner of the business, the CEO is the
only person the CFO works for. In some ways, this situation is easier for CFOs, as
they have only one relationship to manage and one person to keep happy as
opposed to the multiple relationships that exist in the situation described
previously.

The challenge that can be faced by CFOs working for a single person is that
they have only one person to deal with on all the issues, and there is no
opportunity to get other points of view involved in making decisions. Some
CFOs find that working with an owner-manager can be a challenge, especially
when they face a "my way or the highway" attitude from the CEO.

CFOs who have dealt with owner-managers in previous career situations
understand the dynamics that are involved with this situation, accept it, and
know how to make the best of this situation. When CFOs who have previously
worked in collaborative environments accept roles where they are working
directly with an owner-manager, they may be surprised by the cultural
difference they face.

CFOs working with an owner-manager need to ensure they are managing
the CEO's expectations. CFOs should ensure that they are spending a good
amount of time becoming familiar with the needs and desires of the CEO,
engaging regularly in conversations with him about the business and the
challenges being faced. When a CFO really understands the motivations and
needs of the CEO and where he wants to take the business, the CFO can provide
the support and assistance needed to give the CEO comfort and move the
business along the plan to further success.

Family Business

The dynamics of a family business can be very special. If you have never
been involved in a family business before, imagine all the challenges that a

family has. These can include, but are certainly not limited to, rivalry, jealousy, favoritism, deceit, and generational misunderstandings. Now take these family issues, add money and positions of power, and you have a family business.

If you have been involved with this type of business before, I'm certain you have your own stories to tell. When you are the CFO in this type of business and you are not a family member, you will find yourself in the middle. I was at a conference recently with a CFO and asked her where she disappeared to during the day. She told me she had to go back to the office to settle a dispute with the brothers who ran the business. She gave them 30 minutes to get their point across and then made the decision for them.

Your situation may not be like this CFO's, but you need to be aware of the challenges this kind of company faces.

It is necessary to understand the power dynamics involved in this situation, both in terms of the family members who work in the business as well as the family members who are not involved in the day-to-day but are shareholders. The balancing acts that a CFO has to do can make the job of a circus tightrope walker look easy in comparison. Building trust in this setting requires a deep understanding of those running the company and a commitment to continue to deliver to their expectations.

The good news is that I have seen many CFOs thrive in this type of environment because they enjoy the stimulation, revel in being the calm voice in the storm, and appreciate the value that they bring to what can be a dysfunctional atmosphere.

Business Unit

Companies of a certain size can only get to that size when they have multiple business units. In these companies, while the corporate head office may run on a structure where the CFO reports to a CEO, board, and investors, the CFOs at the business units that are part of this company operate with a different structure.

In a business unit environment, the CFO usually reports to the CEO of the business unit, who is sometimes referred to as the General Manager or another company-specific title. The CFO's function in a business unit is to support the financial operations of the business unit. This CFO does not have all the responsibilities of a corporate CFO. In many cases, business unit functions such as treasury are managed and controlled by the head office. Some functions, such as accounts payable, accounts receivable, payables, payroll, and even general ledger accounting, may be part of a shared services function within the corporate group and not under the direct control and supervision of the business unit CFO.

Based on this description, the CFO Relationship Map for the business unit CFO can look very different from the map depicted in Chapter 8. One unique feature of the relationships for business unit CFOs is that, in many cases, they report not only to the business unit CFO but also to the corporate CFO. Where this is the case, the CFO needs to balance the needs and requirements of his CEO with the desires and wishes of the corporate CFO.

Building trust and managing the expectations of both of these bosses is important to the success of this lucky CFO. Knowing these individuals well, understanding their motivations, and ensuring that both are kept happy will contribute to continued success. This business unit finance leader needs to constantly be aware that the needs and requirements of both the business unit CEO and the corporate CFO may clash and put him in a difficult position. The business unit CFO needs to manage and navigate the storms that come when agendas conflict to benefit and succeed in the short and long term.

Not-for-Profits

Not-for-profit organizations have unique characteristics that differentiate them from the corporate business model and the standard CFO Relationship Map. Not-for-profit organizations come in different sizes and structures, each of them with their own exceptional features. Many people think of not-for-profits as charitable organizations, but they can include enterprises that are as diverse as unions, cooperatives, and government entities.

While all not-for-profits will have a CEO (although titles will differ widely, the role is the same), their governing structures may or may not resemble a typical Board of Directors, and there may or may not be an ultimate stakeholder that the governing structure answers to. For example, a government entity may be ultimately answerable to another government entity or even the citizens it serves while a charitable organization may not have anyone it is answerable to at the end of the day.

In this type of environment, it is not always clear who the CFO really works for. To be successful, not-for-profit CFOs need to understand who they are working for, develop relationships that engender trust, and continue to manage expectations. If you think that this sounds like an easy task, ask a not-for-profit CFO how difficult this can really be.

Partnerships

Partnerships are similar in many ways to the standard corporate entity that we discussed in the beginning of the chapter. The legal differences between the structures are well known by finance professionals, so we don't need to go into those issues here. The major difference from a relationship map perspective is that the owners of the company hold their investment in a different legal format. From an operating perspective, some partnerships can cause relationship challenges for the CFO.

Professional service partnerships, such as law, accounting, and engineering firms, can sometimes provide additional challenges to their CFOs. While larger firms may not have these issues, smaller or mid-sized partnerships may have to provide their CFOs with a budget for antacid. I have had professional service firm CFOs explain to me that they have felt they were dealing with a multiheaded monster where everyone was the boss. For professional service firm CFOs to succeed, they need to build trust and deliver on the expectations not only of the managing director and the committee but of each of the partners who act outside of the operating structure set for the firm.

Another partnership that can cause grief for the CFO is the corporate partnership. While the legal structure may be an actual partnership, joint venture, or other setup, it can be similar to the business unit situation described previously, except that instead of reporting to one corporate head office, the CFO will have to report to two or more corporate offices. Again, this situation can be very challenging for the keeper of the finances.

No matter what the specifics of the situation that CFOs find themselves in, they will always have to report to someone. CFOs must always be aware of who they are responsible to and come up with a way to ensure they develop trust with these people and manage their expectations. When Chief Financial Officers keep these people satisfied, they have achieved an important requirement for their success.

CONCLUSION

- We reviewed the CFO's relationship with the Chief Executive Officer, some of the challenges faced by the CFO, and strategies to make the best out of this very important relationship.
- We spoke about the multiple relationships that CFOs have with their boards, how to come up with an effective approach to manage expectations, and key people on the board who need extra special attention.

- We explained why investors need to be considered as a group the CFO works for, the importance of having excellent relations with investors, and ideas on proactive approaches for working with investors.
- We prepared a quick checklist to help you position your relationships with the CEO, board, and investors that can help you identify a plan of action to improve these important relationships.
- We discussed that CFOs always report to someone and gave examples of situations where companies did not deal with the standard CEO, board, and investor dynamic.

The CFO is *a* boss, but never *the* boss. When CFOs build, develop, and nurture excellent relationships with the people they work for, they are paving their own road to success at their employer. Spending time and effort to ensure that these important people are happy and satisfied with your efforts is an important and necessary investment of time for the CFO. In many instances, the CFO has many bosses. When CFOs help them succeed, they will reap the rewards.

CHAPTER TEN

Relationships with Fellow Executives

N THIS CHAPTER, WE continue the discussion about Chief Financial Officer (CFO) relationships by focusing on the people whom you work with, your fellow executives.

Unlike the relationships you have with the people you work for, the people you work with are your peers. In many companies, executives who report to the CEO have the same level of responsibility—they run one department or group of the company and they report to the CEO on their area of accountability. Some companies may have different levels of executives reporting to executives who report to the CFO. No matter how your company has structured the executive reporting diagram, the functions of a company can be divided into two areas: operating and support.

Operating functions can be understood as areas of the business that deal directly with the corporate objectives. These groups vary based on what the company does, but can include areas such as Sales, Production, Design, and Customer Service. Finance, Human Resources, Marketing, and Information Technology (IT) are examples of functions in a business that are necessary to support business operations. This division of functions between operating and support is a construct of my imagination. I have broken this down for the purposes of simplicity and discussion. In your business, Marketing and Sales might be one function. Is this an operating function or a support function? It doesn't really matter. What matters to the company you work for is whether the department is effective and helping achieve corporate objectives such as revenue growth and profitability.

As the executive in charge of the finance function, you need to develop strong and effective relationships with the executives in charge of the other functions in your organization. In your role to support the business from the finance perspective, you can only have the biggest impact on the entire business if you support *all* the functions in your business and the executives who manage them. If each business function is successful, the business will be successful, and so will you as CFO.

In this chapter, I will identify some important business functions that finance has relationships with and strategies for getting the most out of these relationships to allow for overall success. Your business may or may not have these functions. You may have other functions not mentioned that you, as CFO, need to get the best out of. The principles in this chapter will apply to all your relationships, no matter which function or executive you have to take care of at your firm.

HUMAN RESOURCES

Business needs two types of resources to be able to accomplish its goals: financial and human. No business can exist with only one of these assets. Finance and human resources are two support functions that are essential to the proper functioning of any business. Yet, because they are support functions, many people see them as less critical to the business than operating functions such as Sales or Production. Many finance and human resources (HR) professionals have shared their frustrations with me that because they are supporting the operations of the business, they do not get the visibility and respect of the revenue-generating areas of the business. In many organizations, Finance and HR are seen as cost centers and not profit centers. Successful companies know that all functions need to add significant value to the business in a collaborative effort, and this includes the finance and HR functions.

Challenges between Finance and Human Resources

Finance and HR are both critical to the proper functioning of any business. Both functions need to work together for the benefit of the company, yet often they do not.

In 2011, I surveyed CFOs about their relationships with HR and blogged the results. What I found most interesting was that CFOs did not feel they were getting enough value from their relationships with HR. Of those surveyed, most CFOs said they want both functional (day-to-day) tasks and strategic and long-term value from their HR groups. Only half of these CFOs felt they were getting an appropriate level of support from their human resources groups on day-to-day tasks and long-term strategic value.

Throughout my career I have heard CFOs and other finance executives express their frustration with their colleagues in Human Resources. This has always intrigued me over the years, and in fact was the impetus for my development of the CFO Relationship Map. The reasons that finance did not get along with HR varied from "They don't understand our business" to "They waste their time and don't accomplish anything." I have heard some doozies over the years, and do not feel comfortable sharing some of the more memorable ones. I do realize that these expressions of frustration may not have been factually correct, but for these finance executives, perception was reality.

Why are Finance and Human Resources, pillars of support in any company, not able to get along?

Financial capital and human capital are two essential resources for the proper functioning of any business. I see Finance and HR as two sides of the same coin. They are interlinked and related, and each has an impact on the other side. Costs related to people are most often the largest financial costs in most companies. With Finance responsible for managing costs and HR responsible for managing people, this relationship is a conflict waiting to happen.

While clashes between these two groups are almost inevitable, it does not have to be so. This is where you come in as CFO. Applying the four elements of building a successful relationship with HR can make a big difference. (See Chapter 8 to review Elements of Relationship Management.)

Relationship Building with HR

How well do you really know the executive in charge of Human Resources? When was the last time you spent any time developing a personal relationship with this individual? Do you know the key issues facing him and what makes him lose sleep at night? Does he know yours?

If you do not have a great relationship with HR, you need to start by getting to know your fellow executive, and he needs to start getting to know you.

If you do not know your HR executive well, you can always start at the beginning. If you don't like your HR executive, you may not be able to start over from the beginning. But you should at least try to build a rapport with him. If you don't like each other, you will have a very hard time building trust, which is essential for the delivery part of the relationship and managing expectations. You can always try to get the individual replaced, but that may not be realistic, practical, or appropriate.

Building trust with HR should start with agreeing on objectives that you can cooperate on. There are many places and projects that require the cooperation of Finance and HR, and you're probably working on a few of them right now.

It is not enough that the two senior executives from HR and Finance know, like, and trust each other. As leaders, you need to have your teams work together and begin to know, like, and trust each other, as well. Working with your HR peer on finding ways to collaborate better will make both of your jobs easier. One-on-one relationships are always easier to build than relationships between teams. When the tone from the top is one of friendship and cooperation on business objectives, your teams have the right role models for making this important relationship work. Both of you will have to be involved to ensure that your teams are making the necessary efforts.

Main Challenge with HR: Budget

The budget process is a critical point where the interests of finance and human resources connect. If your company has an annual budget process, speak with your fellow HR executive prior to the process starting, or, preferably, following the finalization of your annual process. Work to understand the challenges your teams have both faced in the past. Listen to the frustrations faced on the other side and explain what issues your team faced when interacting with the HR group during this annual process. By putting the issues both sides have faced previously on the table, you can work to better understand each other and find the common ground necessary for moving forward to build mutual trust and deliver results based on agreed-upon expectations.

HR Supporting Finance

As CFO, you run a team that supports the business. Your team is composed of people, also known as *human resources*. To run your team efficiently and effectively, you need the best HR support possible to meet the corporate challenges you have been given. As CFO, you can only be as successful as your team allows you to be. Having a great team will help you become a great CFO.

Human resources professionals are trained and experienced in dealing with hiring, retaining, and developing talent. You need to hire, retain, and develop talent. What a perfect opportunity for you to gain significant value from your HR group.

Many CFOs and finance executives complain that they don't get the support they need from HR. They tell me that they are hiring their own talent and dealing with issues of development and retention by themselves. I am told that they do this by themselves because they cannot trust HR to deliver for them.

Would it not be wonderful if you could rely on the support of HR to help you accomplish your goals? Many finance executives would agree with this statement, but feel that it is just easier to address the problem of talent acquisition, retention, and development by themselves as opposed to trying to develop the HR relationship.

One thing I love about finance professionals is their tenacity in solving the problems facing them using whatever limited resources they have. But sometimes, their MacGyver-like attitudes are really not the most appropriate solution for themselves or their companies. I encourage CFOs to make the effort to develop a better relationship with HR so that they can benefit directly and become a better and more successful CFO.

Finance Supporting HR

To be able to get HR professionals to assist finance professionals in becoming the best they can be, it is worthwhile for finance to invest in and support the HR team to help it become the best it can be.

Many experienced finance professionals believe that a big challenge that HR specialists face is that they do not really understand the financial aspects of their own businesses. Rather than grumble and mumble that HR does not understand the business and how the company makes money, use this as an opportunity to get your team to get to know the people who work in HR.

Consider creating a financial training program for HR to help these professionals better understand how your business makes money and what the financial key performance indicators that are bandied about in your culture really mean. Ask what areas of finance they would like to understand better. Nurture a culture of openness between your groups that will allow people to feel comfortable asking questions to better understand the financial realities of

How Strong Is Your Human Resources Relationship?

Rate the strength of your HR relationship:

Very weak   _____
Weak   _____
Neither   _____
Strong   _____
Very strong   _____

How much room for improvement do you have in your HR relationship?

A lot   _____
A little   _____
It is good, but could be better   _____
It couldn't be better   _____

Areas for improvement:

1. _____
2. _____
3. _____

Detail your plan for improving your HR relationship:

_____
_____
_____

your organization and how they impact the company's most expensive resource.

When the people in the Human Resources department better understand the role of finance in meeting corporate objectives and can translate what they do into a language that Finance can understand, both you and the executive in charge of HR benefit directly, not to mention that your company as a whole benefits, as well.

INFORMATION TECHNOLOGY

Imagine business today without Information Technology (IT). It is not possible for any organization to function without IT. Information Technology is a key support for any business. In an ever-changing world with continuous improvements in technology and short periods of obsolescence, costly investments are needed on a continuous basis. All companies, no matter their size, need to deal with IT issues. Once companies reach a certain size, IT becomes a department of its own with an executive in charge, a significant headcount, and a large budget for IT hardware and software, as well as a project arm to ensure that the changing needs of the business are met.

Like Finance, IT is a necessary support function that is a cost center. Even in companies that deliver IT services as a line of business, IT is a necessary internal support function to ensure that the business can run smoothly.

Challenges between Finance and Information Technology

In most businesses, support functions compete for prominence and budget resources. One cannot say that Finance is necessary and IT is not, nor can either Finance or IT proclaim that it is more important than the other. An effective and efficient IT function is just as critical for a company as finance is. Finance has its own goals, and IT does, as well. It is in the difference between these goals that conflict arises.

The IT group is given the task to support the business by ensuring that the company has the technology it needs to be effective and competitive. Finance believes that IT, in its desire to help the company be more effective and competitive, considers the cost of Information Technology initiatives less important than finding technology solutions that meet these goals. Finance professionals may believe that IT would spend what it wanted to if it could, because it considers that throwing resources at challenges faced by the business is the best way to solve them. When you add to this the experience that finance people have of seeing IT projects started but not completed, with significant resources wasted, it is difficult for professionals on the finance side of the corporate table to believe everything they hear from IT.

People in IT would likely say that the role of finance in their business is to say *no*. With Finance as the keeper of the corporate purse strings and charged with managing costs, it is easier for Finance to say *no* to great IT ideas and solutions that solve real business problems than to take the time to understand the value these expenditures will bring.

The challenges that exist between IT and Finance are easy to understand, yet hard to solve. The only way Finance and IT can work together to best support the company is for the senior executives of each group to build a solid relationship based on mutual respect.

Relationship Building with IT

Once you appreciate that this is an important relationship that needs to be nurtured and developed, you can make the difference by planning your approach and acting on it. How would you assess your relationship with IT? Is there room for improvement? What is the biggest challenge you face with IT? What does IT think about you as CFO and your finance team?

Take the time to not only develop your relationship with the senior IT executive, but also encourage the development of knowledge, respect, and trust between your teams. Developing strong interdepartmental bonds can only take place when the heads of those departments make visible and sincere efforts to challenge the status quo and create opportunities to agree on more and work on finding solutions when they don't agree.

Remember, you need IT and IT needs you. Creating conflict with IT or ignoring the relationship doesn't help you meet your objectives. Make the effort.

Main Challenge with IT: New Projects

Ongoing, regular IT service is a critical part of running a company. Finance will usually not have an issue with these costs, as they have been ongoing and there is a historical cost/value perspective. Finance understands that IT needs to keep delivering what it has delivered in the past.

Where conflict often arises between IT and Finance is in the area of new projects. Situations like enterprise resource planning (ERP) implementations, new systems purchases, technology replacement, and any large, new IT project that will require a significant investment of dollars and people is a cause for friction between these two groups.

The way to move beyond the inherent challenges in a new IT project is for both sides to work together from the beginning. IT has to take the time to explain the need, make the economic case, and request input from Finance in developing a value proposition that makes sense to Finance and the rest of the business. Finance needs to be involved from the early stages of the new project so it can understand the value proposition to the business. Finance should help develop the business case in conjunction with the IT team and provide options for ensuring the project is successful and on budget.

Success in the preparation, planning, and implementation of a new IT project can only be achieved when the CFO and Chief Information Officer (or whatever your top IT executive is called) show leadership to their teams by working together and being respectful and supportive of each other's needs.

IT Supporting Finance

Look at your desk. The computer that is sitting on it runs properly because of IT. The programs that run on the computer that you rely upon for your personal time management, your analysis tools, and your access to corporate information as well as your ability to communicate with others are all working because IT supports you. Your smartphone connects to your corporate network and gives you access to information you need when you're on the go because IT made it happen and continues to ensure that it works properly. The work that you and your finance team do to support the company could not happen without your IT group.

If I were to ask you if your technology runs the way you want it to, you would probably be able to give me examples of what you would like improved. You might also be able to give me an example of a project that was important to Finance that was started but not finished on time or is still sitting in limbo after two years.

As CFO, you need technology to run efficiently and effectively; you cannot do your job without it. You need to build an excellent relationship with the IT department, not only to ensure that the company as a whole has the information it needs to help make great decisions; you and your team need this as well. Developing a strong relationship with IT can only work in your interest.

Finance Supporting IT

Why should your finance team, comprised of very busy individuals, make the effort to provide value to colleagues in IT?

IT needs your help on many fronts to achieve its objectives. The IT team wants to bring the best value to its projects. They are sensitive to cost, and want to ensure they are spending the right amounts in the right places. They need to understand the corporate objectives, what impact their work has on those objectives, and how the financial components of those objectives are directly affected by the work they do. Given their need for Finance support and your need for IT support, it only makes sense to find a way to work well together for the benefit of everyone.

Think about how you can better support IT in your company. Does IT need help with budgeting? Does it need assistance when preparing a new project to ensure the financial aspects of the business case make sense? Are supplier terms or costs an issue that they would like to address but need some guidance from your experienced group? You will not know how you can help IT if you don't ask.

How Strong Is Your IT Relationship?

Rate the strength of your IT relationship:

Very weak _____
Weak _____
Neither _____
Strong _____
Very strong _____

How much room for improvement do you have in your IT relationship?

A lot _____
A little _____
It is good, but could be better _____
It cannot be better _____

Areas for improvement:

1. _____
2. _____
3. _____

Detail your plan for improving your IT relationship:

_____
_____
_____

MARKETING

Marketing can be the most mysterious of all business functions for the finance professional. While Human Resources and Information Technology are groups that finance people can understand logically, Marketing is a creative function that does not logically compute for most finance professionals. Even the sales function makes more sense to a person with a finance personality and background.

As mentioned previously, while I consider marketing to be a support function, it can be argued that it is an operations function. In the end, it doesn't matter whether it is support or operations. What does matter is that marketing is an important function for all businesses. Some businesses have developed a dedicated marketing function to support sales. Others incorporate marketing into the Sales group.

The reason I want to discuss marketing with my finance audience is because it is often difficult for finance professionals to properly understand. If you say that you understand marketing well, I will believe you. But believe me when I say that many of your finance peers are at a loss to really explain what marketing does and how it does it.

Challenges between Finance and Marketing

Finance and Marketing each know that the other is important, if not critical, to the success of the business. Yet, the biggest challenge in the relationship between Finance and Marketing is that each has a lack of understanding of what the other does.

The task of marketing is to communicate the value of the company's products or services to customers and potential customers in a way that supports the eventual sale of the product. This process, if accomplished well, makes it easier for the company to sell and make money. Marketing is an indirect support function (i.e., supporting the sales effort) and often it is difficult to identify a direct link between the resources spent and the eventual sale. Finance professionals must be comfortable with the notion of spending money to make money. For this group, it is often a challenge to understand how spending more marketing dollars will increase the top and bottom lines.

Marketing people are often creative types who look to raise their organization's visibility and drive specific behaviors among their target market. According to Kent Huffman, Chief Marketing Officer at Bearcom Wireless and author of *8 Mandates for Social Media Marketing Success* (C-Suite Press, 2012), many marketing professionals are more concerned about the attractiveness of a website or the creativeness of an advertising campaign than they are about their impact on the bottom or top line.

The basic differences between how finance and marketing professionals think can be cause for a serious disconnect. Huffman says that finance people typically are more left-brained and marketing folks more right-brained, whether by nature, training, or both. We have talked about the need for senior finance professionals to move out of the comfort zone where they were trained to be purely analytical and embrace a more well-rounded business approach to make a difference. Just as you, the finance executive, need to be more holistic in your approach to business, so does the marketing professional. Just because your basic instinct is to think and live in your own preferred brain hemisphere, it doesn't mean that you can't learn and appreciate what the other perspective brings to the table.

Relationship Building with Marketing

Unlike when dealing with other functions where it is easy for the CFO to understand the value they bring to the table, the first step in building your relationship with Marketing is to better appreciate the significance of marketing to your business.

Make the effort to get to know the Chief Marketing Executive at your business and work to understand the challenges this individual faces as well as the value he brings to the table. You may need to put your definition of value on hold while you listen to your marketing peer. Spend time and ask questions to understand what gets him excited, and what challenging projects he is working on, and listen to examples of recent successes that he is proud of. Asking questions and listening to the answers will begin to build the elements required for success in this relationship.

Before dismissing marketing as an area that is not worth spending your relationship development time on, take the logical step of understanding that demand for the products and services your business offers needs to be generated somewhere. You may not understand fully how demand is generated and how interest in your company and product or service is created, but believe that your Marketing group is doing something right. Understanding your entire business, including the value that marketing brings to the table, is an important investment in your success as a CFO as well as your overall business.

Main Challenge with Marketing: Value

Investments made by companies in marketing activities are perceived to have a value; otherwise, the company would not spend money on them. Yet the biggest challenge Marketing has is being able to prove its value. The question that is continually asked of marketing groups is "Are we getting value for our money?" In tough economic times, when costs across an enterprise are being challenged and looked at closely, Marketing faces an ongoing battle to prove its worth.

In 2007, CFO magazine published an article called "Finance vs. Marketing," by Joseph McCafferty (www.cfo.com/article.cfm/9059269). The article begins, "Companies are still struggling to measure their returns on marketing investments . . . " and goes on to explain the differences in perceived value of marketing efforts by Finance and Marketing. The article states: "Lack of cooperation between marketing and finance is also hindering efforts to develop ROI measures. Just 19 percent of the finance executives surveyed by MMA (Marketing Management Analytics) report full cooperation, while more than

8 percent report frequent conflicts with marketing over budget and strategy and another 13 percent report no meaningful relationship at all."

In 2013, the challenge of measuring marketing value continues. Social media has grown in importance for marketing departments since the 2007 article, yet "a lot of people struggle to measure the impact of social media," says Bearcom Wireless's Kent Huffman. When it comes to branding, Huffman says that measuring the impact of marketing continues to be a challenge for marketing professionals. If Marketing cannot properly explain the value of what it spends all its working hours on, how can Finance properly understand the value of the continuous investments made by the Marketing group?

Marketing Supporting Finance

Marketing has the ability to directly influence the sphere of Finance in areas that are important to it, especially for publicly listed companies. Strong brand awareness can lead to more investor interest and a higher share price. A well-branded company and product can also lead to increased revenue and profitability, although the finance mind-set would only be able to buy into the success with confidence after the fact.

A well-rounded and effective finance team has leaders and individuals who understand the business they work in very well. Finance professionals need to be able to properly appreciate not only the technical aspects, such as how a product is manufactured or how the customer gets delivery of the goods, but also what drives the customer to be interested in what the company has to sell and how the company creates and meets demand for what it is selling. The more that Finance is involved in marketing, the better Finance understands the value, both measurable and not, that Marketing brings to the company.

Finance Supporting Marketing

Finance can help Marketing understand and apply the concepts of profitability and data analytics to measure value from marketing activities. One way the CFO can make a difference to Marketing is to transfer one of the group's most talented up-and-comers into Marketing for a rotation. Another option is to create crossfunctional teams between Finance and Marketing that can support accountability of major marketing efforts. The analytical skills that finance professionals have mix very well in an environment like marketing that generates a lot of data. Having your finance professional show marketing peers how they can analyze the data to develop useable and valuable information will support Marketing in a meaningful way.

Huffman says that Finance can help Marketing better understand its role in influencing corporate profitability. He says that marketing people "tend to be more in tune with the creative side of marketing and less in tune with the analytical side, and they may not even care about the financial impact of their actions, unless their bonus program relies on it." Financial training can make a big difference to the Marketing group. The CFO can also get the buy-in of the Chief Marketing Officer to agree to base a portion of the group's compensation on profitability or other relevant financial objectives.

Huffman also said that he believes that Finance can help marketing peers even further by helping them understand how to analyze the potential risk and reward of any planned marketing initiative before they make the decision to heavily invest in that initiative.

How Strong Is Your Marketing Relationship?

Rate the strength of your marketing relationship:

Very weak	_____
Weak	_____
Neither	_____
Strong	_____
Very strong	_____

How much room for improvement do you have in your marketing relationship?

A lot	_____
A little	_____
It is good, but could be better	_____
It cannot be better	_____

Areas for improvement:

1. _____
2. _____
3. _____

Detail your plan for improving your marketing relationship:

_____
_____
_____

SALES

The sales function of your business needs to be successful for your business to be successful. Sales is one of those departments that gets lots of attention and resources because it is so critical to the well-being of your organization. Finance understands and appreciates the value that Sales brings to the table, but the relationship between these two functions can be strained by conflicting values and interests.

The size and cost of your sales organization depends on the channels though which you make your sales and the complexity of the sales process for your products or services. The larger and more multifaceted your sales team is, the more important your relationship is with your senior sales executive. As CFO, you have a vested interested in increased revenue that is profitable. Having a strong relationship with Sales can allow Finance to have an impact on the top line as well as the bottom line.

Challenges between Finance and Sales

The sales group is challenged to maintain and increase revenue. Finance, on the other hand, is charged with increasing profitability and cash and controlling assets. Finance professionals who have gone through audit training clearly understand that these two mandates have the ability to clash with each other.

The sales department of any company gets its recognition from continuous success in meeting and exceeding sales targets. Compensation for many sales teams is structured to weigh heavily on such success. "More" is the basis of motivating the entire department. This environment, if not carefully monitored, can lead to sales that are not profitable, not deliverable, or not even collectible. In complex sales environments like technology that include software licensing as well as service commitments, poorly structured deals can cause headaches for Finance, especially when it comes to the ability to recognize revenue for such sales.

Your experience may have shown that people working in Sales see Finance as a roadblock that limits their ability to sell. Credit limits and collection issues with some customers can cause a salesperson to blame Finance for not making the sale. As CFO, you may even have experienced pressure from the head of Sales to lift credit limits to be able to make an important sale.

These are only some of the challenges that can have an impact on the relationship between Sales and Finance. When both groups have a good working relationship with each other, they are able to minimize situations where their interests clash and have an even greater positive impact on the success of their business.

Relationship Building with Sales

The sales function is easy for finance professionals to understand. Sales is measurable and has a significant and visible impact on the company.

When Sales and Finance do not have an excellent relationship, the company suffers. This is unfortunate, because if Sales and Finance have a good working relationship, the company can achieve even higher levels of success. Finance and Sales both gain when they treat each other as partners as opposed to adversaries.

Do you know what is causing the head of Sales to lose sleep at night? Are you aware of what the sales pipeline looks like and the probability of all the deals really closing? Has the chief sales executive discussed with you upcoming plans for entering new markets or selling new product lines? Have you been asked to assist your chief sales executive with reviewing the compensation plan for the sales team with the goal of improving sales, profitability, and collections? These are just some of the areas you and your sales peer can collaborate on if you develop a strong, effective relationship.

Main Challenge with Sales: Processes

Salespeople enjoy getting their customers to say *yes*. Salespeople do not enjoy the processes that Finance cannot live without. Filling out forms, opening accounts, and recording the sale in the system properly are all things that most salespeople do not enjoy doing. Salespeople are happy to take an order, even if the customer has not paid for previous purchases on a timely basis. They get upset when customers have reached their credit limits or the account has been put on hold by the credit manager. Sales professionals are never happy with the amount or the timing of their commission check, and are always ready to fault Finance for sticking to process and procedures.

Sure, finance controls are necessary, but do salespeople really understand why they exist and the potential consequences to the company and to themselves if they are not followed? This and other areas of conflict can be minimized by opening the lines of communication between the groups and by the leaders of the Sales and Finance teams creating a tone from the top where each group accords importance and respect to the other group.

Sales Supporting Finance

Finance is heavily involved with the financial aspect of the sales process. These areas can include credit approval, invoicing, and collection, depending on the nature of the business. Sales can have a positive impact on the Finance group if salespeople understand the importance of these areas for Finance and the impact on the company if policies are not followed properly.

Another place where the sales group can support Finance is in the area of budgets and cash flows. In order for Finance to be able to create financial plans for the future, Finance needs to understand what revenue will be in the future. The sales group can support Finance by providing the finance team with appropriate estimates that have a realistic chance of reflecting the eventual reality. It may be difficult to forecast revenue, but the importance of projecting these numbers cannot be overstated.

Finance Supporting Sales

Finance has a vested interested in the ongoing and continued success of the sales team. While there certainly are points of conflict with Sales, these are procedural issues that can be smoothed over once the relationship moves to the value-added phase. Finance can support Sales by doing things like minimizing delays in the approval of new accounts and keeping the salesperson involved and up to date on accounts with collection issues. Finance can also make a personal difference to sales professionals by creating a method that easily explains how they are being paid their sales commissions.

In some companies, making a sale is a complex process. Imagine for a moment that your company builds a very expensive product to the order and specifications of your customer. You may have a price list for such products, but because your product is so specific to your client and because you do not sell a large volume of these products, pricing and terms can vary greatly from sale to sale. When you consider that each sale is structured differently, each sale is critically important to your bottom line. The expertise and experience that Finance can bring to the negotiating table can help Sales maximize each sale.

Commission structure is another area where Finance can make a big difference to the Sales group. For commissions to be most effective, they need to motivate salespeople to sell more profitably. Commission structures that do not take into account the profitability of the product being sold can have a significant negative impact on margins or even lead to products being sold at a loss. Finance can support the analysis and creation of a performance-based

How Strong Is Your Sales Relationship?

Rate the strength of your sales relationship:

Very weak   _____
Weak   _____
Neither   _____
Strong   _____
Very strong   _____

How much room for improvement do you have in your sales relationship?

A lot   _____
A little   _____
It is good, but could be better   _____
It cannot be better   _____

Areas for improvement:

1. _____
2. _____
3. _____

Detail your plan for improving your sales relationship:

_____
_____
_____

compensation package for the sales team that can encourage more sales that are more profitable.

 PRODUCTION

Support functions are common across different businesses and industries. Operating functions at different businesses are not the same. They depend on the type of business and industry the company functions in. Not every company has a production function. I am using production for CFO relationship purposes to provide an example of an operations function for a complex business. Again, the examples in this chapter have been provided as much to learn about the specific function as to provide examples for you to learn from that can be applied to your CFO relationships.

If your business includes Production as a significant component of your value chain, you know that the financial impact of this operation is significant to your business. In the production process, where costs are key and investment is critical, the value that you as CFO bring to the table can be significant. When Finance is involved and making a difference to Production, your entire company benefits.

Challenges between Finance and Production

Production is challenged with the task of manufacturing products within the constraints of a limited timeframe with maximum quality and minimum cost. To be able to achieve this combination of tasks, Production may need to invest significant financial resources. When it comes to production activities, Finance is focused on maintaining and minimizing costs, as well as the investment decisions made for production activities. The interests of Finance and Production intersect in the areas of investments and costs.

Both groups need to work together on the investment process and on costing issues. This interaction can create challenges for their relationship because of their unique perspective on these issues. Conflict will not necessarily arise, but it takes effort for each group to understand the other's point of view and biases and to be able to work together for the overall benefit of the company.

Relationship Building with Production

While Sales is important to the top line of a business, it is in Production that profit is made. Getting the best out of production costs is a key component in being able to maximize profit. The production processes in a company are far from simple. They are a complex set of functions that are impacted by situations that can be controlled and conditions that cannot. To be able to build a solid relationship with Production, Finance needs to understand the difficult challenges faced by this group.

When was the last time you, as CFO, took a tour of your company's production facilities? Do you know where they are? Do you know what they produce? Do you know the challenges and opportunities of each plant? Do you understand the cost drivers that have an impact on the bottom line? Are you able to identify the areas where investments will have a significant return? Do you know which products are more profitable than others? Wouldn't knowing this information allow you to add value to the work your colleagues in Production do?

Making the investment in a strong relationship with your chief production executive will allow you to add value for that individual and the department while helping you achieve your own goals. Imagine the value that can be created for your company in partnership with your peer in Production. Invest in this relationship and produce the rewards.

Main Challenge with Production: Costing

The total costs of production are relatively simple to identify. Applying the total costs to each individual unit produced can be a very complex process. There are a number of theories in management accounting as to how to best allocate costs of production to product. The challenge in any environment is to find the best method that is most appropriate to your environment and to apply it regularly and consistently.

As CFO, your management accounting staff will be the front line in being able to figure out what individual costs really are. You have a vested interest in creating and maintaining a positive relationship between the members of your finance team and the production crew. Your team's ability to understand how production really works, and the challenge faced therein, will allow them to be in a good position to properly assess true costs at the product level. Your team members should be creating costing information with input from the production team members at all appropriate levels.

In the ideal situation, the costing of your products should be driven by an information system overseen by your team members and created from manufacturing data obtained in integrated manner. Even in today's information age, too many costing environments rely on manual inputs and estimates to create a guesstimate of actual costs. As CFO, you have the responsibility to ensure that the costing information you receive is reliable and timely to be able to help your company make great business decisions. Only by creating an excellent relationship with your production team can you achieve this kind of value.

Production Supporting Finance

When Finance and Production have a good working relationship, the production team supports its finance counterparts by giving them the information they need when they need it. If this sounds a little too simplistic, imagine for a moment a situation where Production is not cooperating with Finance. You may even have experienced circumstances like this yourself.

The information you need may be related to understanding costing of product, margin analysis, costs of waste, or labor efficiency. Production is an expensive process in your business, and the better your relationship with Production, the easier it will be for Finance to do its job.

Finance Supporting Production

In a company that focuses on manufacturing product, the production team must be successful for the finance team to be successful. Finance has the experience and knowledge to make a difference to Production and ultimately the entire business.

How Strong Is Your Production Relationship?

Rate the strength of your production relationship:

Very weak   _____
Weak   _____
Neither   _____
Strong   _____
Very strong   _____

How much room for improvement do you have in your production relationship?

A lot   _____
A little   _____
It is good, but could be better   _____
It cannot be better   _____

Areas for improvement:

1. _____
2. _____
3. _____

Detail your plan for improving your production relationship:

_____
_____
_____

Production needs to continue to meet its quality initiatives and production targets; it is responsible for ensuring that product manufacturing costs remain in check. When the production group takes all these challenges seriously, Finance can assist with cost and profitability analysis that will help support Production in coming to profitable business decisions on an ongoing basis.

Finance has the skills and abilities to support Production with important future-oriented decisions. Investment decisions are a key area where Finance is in a good position to assist. Should the company invest in a new plant? What should be done with the old plant? Does the business need to buy a major new piece of equipment? Will it be profitable? Should it subcontract manufacturing of its product or key components of its product? When does such a decision make most sense financially? These decisions cannot be made by Production alone. Finance has the ability to help make great investment decisions.

Whether Production needs assistance with its day-to-day objectives or planning for future success, a strong partnership with Finance can help the group achieve its goals.

 ## CONCLUSION

- ▪ We stated the importance to CFOs of having effective relationships with their executive peers.
- ▪ We reviewed the CFO's relationship with Human Resources and identified strategies for getting the best out of this relationship.
- ▪ We discussed how Finance and Information Technology need each other to achieve their goals.
- ▪ We identified that often Marketing and Finance each do not understand what the other does and how to break down that barrier to provide each other with much-needed value.
- ▪ We talked about the importance of the sales function to the business, how Finance can make it better, and how Sales can help Finance with its concerns.
- ▪ We explained the challenges that Production and Finance have with each other and how they can solve their issues and benefit each other and the company.
- ▪ We listed important points that will help you work to identify the status of your current interaction with each of these executive peers and help guide you to create a plan of action to improve these relationships.

Your business is made up of different components that need to work cohesively with each other in order to reach and exceed your corporate objectives. Each part of the business needs to work together. As the leader of Finance, you have the ability to make a difference to the entire business by developing excellent relationships with the executives who lead these other important groups in your business. Making an investment in your relationships with your peers will add tremendous value to the entire business and to your personal success as CFO.

CHAPTER ELEVEN

Relationships with Outsiders

C HAPTERS 9 AND 10 discussed the important relationships you have as Chief Financial Officer (CFO) with the people you work for (Chapter 9) and the people you work with inside your organization (Chapter 10). This chapter speaks to the left side of your relationship map, the people you work with outside your company (see Figure 8.1 for the CFO Relationship Map).

As CFO, you have a number of relationships with people who do not work in your business. The work they do has an important impact on your business. Successful relationships with these individuals are necessary for you to get your job done and be the best CFO you can be. Not only is having a good relationship with these important people necessary, having a difficult relationship with any of these people may lead to significant complications for you and the business you support.

This chapter reviews some key relationships that are common to many businesses. Your important outside relationships may include others that are not discussed in this chapter. Whether the relationships mentioned here apply to you or you have other important relationships, applying the principles and strategies discussed here will make a difference to you, improve the quality and effectiveness of your dealings with these people, and help you become a more successful CFO.

To get the best out of your relationships with people outside your company, remember the four elements of relationship management: knowledge, likability, trust, and expectations (see Chapter 8's Elements of Relationship Management). Working these elements for each of these people will allow you to achieve success with these important relationships.

AUDITORS

Most CFOs do not go through the expense and effort of having their financial statements audited because they want to. They do this because they have to. The financial statement audit of a company is prepared when required by regulators, as is necessary when a company is publicly listed, or when required by investors or lenders to the company. A set of audited financial statements gives assurance to the people reading them that the information they have access to meets certain standards.

Relationship Strategies

Ongoing, regular, two-way communication with your auditor is important. Planning for the audit needs to be communicated by the auditor early enough so that you can be prepared with the information he needs before he needs it. Changes in accounting standards happen on a regular basis, and you rely on your auditors to provide you with updates as well as guidance on how to properly prepare your information in light of these changes. You need to be made aware of concerns that your auditor has as soon as possible so that you can address them.

All of these are important in your relationship with your auditors. If you have a positive, open, and trusting relationship with your auditors, these issues will be dealt with seamlessly. If you have not been able to build mutual trust

> **Relationship tip**: You have your current auditor, and you should build a relationship with this individual. But do not ignore building relationships with others in the audit profession. You may find yourself in a situation where you need your next auditor. It would be helpful if you did not have to start building a brand-new relationship.

and have not been able to deliver based on their expectations, you could find yourself in a troubling situation.

Impact of a Weak Relationship

Audit fees are expensive, and have a tendency to increase annually. When you have a difficult relationship with your auditors, you are not able to communicate properly, schedule work appropriately, and deliver information efficiently. This can cause time delays and lead to additional work by the auditor, which will ultimately result in an increased fee.

A negative relationship with your auditor does not help you with your relationship with the board and the audit committee. Increased conflict, issues that need to be addressed with the audit committee, and bigger fees can adversely affect the reputation you have with the people you work for (see Chapter 9).

Challenges on the audit front can lead to late completion of your audited financial statements. Filing late financial statements can have a negative impact on your share price, on your company's reputation in the market, and with your lenders. This can also have a direct negative impact on your personal reputation in the marketplace.

Impact of a Strong Relationship

An excellent relationship with your auditors can reduce or minimize increases in your audit fee. A strong rapport with your auditor allows for mutual trust to be a key component of your relationship. This trust leads to effective communication and the meeting of each other's expectations regarding the audit. Being able to manage issues on a timely basis and plan for your audit accordingly have an impact on the eventual cost of the audit services provided.

The financial statement audit is a key point of your interaction with the audit committee. Your performance is noted and rated. When an audit runs smoothly and the auditor tells this to the audit committee, your get important brownie points with the board.

While some CFOs may be concerned about what auditors will find, having the auditors looking through your systems and processes can be a good thing. If they find issues that need to be addressed, you can work to correct them and make sure they don't become an issue. Also, when the auditor does not find issues of concern, this can give you and the board comfort that things are working well.

How Strong Is Your Auditor Relationship?

Rate the strength of your auditor relationship:

Very weak   _____
Weak   _____
Neither   _____
Strong   _____
Very strong   _____

How much room for improvement do you have in your auditor relationship?

A lot   _____
A little   _____
It is good, but could be better   _____
It cannot be better   _____

Areas for improvement:

1. _____
2. _____
3. _____

Detail your plan for improving your auditor relationship:

_____
_____
_____

LENDERS

We discussed the CFO's relationship with investors in Chapter 9. Equity investors are only one source for funding for a business. Lenders are another important source of funding for any business. This relationship is fundamentally different from your relationship with investors, although in some cases your equity investor could be providing you with debt, as well.

Debt lenders come in different forms. They can be traditional banks, private equity funds, government entities, asset-based lenders, individuals, and even other businesses. Our conversation today is not about the benefits of one lender versus another. The purpose of this discussion is to discuss strategies for improving the relationship you have with your lenders.

Relationship Strategies

Your lender gives you money (or access to money) not out of the goodness of its heart, but because it wants to make money from its relationship with you. Your borrowing money from the lender will, based on the risk that it faces, make it a certain amount of profit. This profit comes from interest and fees charged to you throughout the period that you are borrowing money.

The key challenge for any lender is making money and limiting the risk it faces that it will lose the funds that your company is holding. A lender feels comfortable making a loan based on what it knows about the business and the reputation and honesty of the people running it. To continue to feel comfortable throughout the period of the loan, the lender asks for specific information and requires that certain criteria be met to continue to extend the loan on the same terms it was originally granted. Lenders use numerical criteria based on financial and other information, called *covenants*, to provide them with assurance that the business is functioning properly and the risk they face is within acceptable limits.

Business is not simple. There are ups and downs in any business, and lenders understand this. However, for trust to grow, lenders need to feel that you (and your company) are being honest regarding the information you provide and that you are keeping them informed about any difficult situations in your company that may affect them. The must feel they understand your plans and forecasts for the future, while getting the results of the past on a timely basis.

Knowledge is a critical lubricant for the successful, ongoing functioning of the lender–borrower relationship. Lenders need to know you before lending you money and must continue to get to know you throughout your relationship. It takes an effort on your part to continue to build this relationship. The more your lenders know you, the better your relationship can be.

Trust is a very important part of a relationship with your lenders. You are holding their money, and they have to trust that you are doing the right things with it. Sharing your information on a timely basis and meeting their expectations for the delivery of information they are interested in, both future-oriented and past financial information, helps your cause. When lenders feel that you are being open, trustworthy, and transparent with them, they are more likely to be helpful if difficult situations arise. As one of my CFO advisors said about his lender:

I advised our bank of a potential loss for the year. The bank was appreciative of not "receiving a surprise" at year-end. At the same time, we were able to get a margin bulge to deal with the temporary situation. My CEO was surprised, impressed, and grateful.

Lenders are in business to make money. If you build trust with them, are open and communicative, and meet their expectations that are set clearly in advance, they will be supportive in helping you make money, too.

Relationships are not built with institutions, but with people at those organizations. As a borrower, the relationship you need to build is with the person or people responsible for your account. It is also helpful to get to know the team members whom your representative works with, and even the person to whom your contact reports. The day you need to speak with your contact will be the day she will be unavailable. You want the others who can help you to know who you are.

Also, as CFO, you may be the key person managing these relationships, or you may have a treasurer who takes care of your company's lenders. Make sure that you are part of your treasurer's relationship building efforts in case one day you need to step in and manage an issue that arises.

Relationship tip: In addition to fostering your relationships with your current lenders, build relationships with other potential lenders. Do not ignore a lender that reaches out to build business with you. Use it as an opportunity to keep your options open for the future should you need a new source of lending or be in a position to replace a current one.

Impact of a Weak Relationship

The most drastic impact of having a challenging relationship with your lender is that it will call its loan. If this happens, it will usually be because the relationship has deteriorated over a period of time. Lenders take such a step when they have no more confidence in your business.

If your company finds itself facing a temporary financial challenge, your lender will be less likely to help if your relationship is fragile. When your rapport with your lender is challenged, it is unlikely that you will be able to secure a new loan for new circumstances.

Impact of a Strong Relationship

When a company faces financially challenging circumstances, a strong relationship built on trust and honesty will lead to better results than a difficult relationship. A strong bond with your lender can allow you to get through difficult circumstances. For example, in temporary situations where, for rational reasons, your company is facing a cash flow challenge, your lenders are more likely to be reasonable and accommodating when you have been sharing information and developing your relationship on an ongoing basis.

In times where it makes sense to look again at the services your lenders offer, either to consolidate the number of institutions you deal with or to negotiate better fees, having a strong relationship with your current lenders will certainly help them consider ways to get you a better deal to keep your business. Also, your reputation as a good company to do business with will make its way through your financial community, including to those that you may consider doing business with in the future.

List Your Key Lending Relationships:	Rate the Strength of Your Lending Relationships:
1. _____	Very weak/Weak/Neither/Strong/Very strong
2. _____	Very weak/Weak/Neither/Strong/Very strong
3. _____	Very weak/Weak/Neither/Strong/Very strong

How much room for improvement do you have in your lending relationships?

A lot	_____
A little	_____
They are good, but could be better	_____
They could not be better	_____

Areas for improvement:

1. _____
2. _____
3. _____

Detail your plan for improving your lending relationships:
_____
_____
_____

Treating your lenders with respect, honesty, and openness is a worthwhile investment of your time and energy as CFO. The benefits to the business are lower costs, better service, and help when you need it most. Building and maintaining strong lending relationships leads directly to more CFO success.

 LAWYERS

We could start this section with lawyer jokes. I would rather begin with a discussion of the value that lawyers bring to a company. Almost every business is a legal creation, whether an incorporation, partnership, cooperative, or joint venture. Lawyers are needed even before a business begins its life. In all aspects of your business, from employment to intellectual property, from contracts to securities and all points in between, legal advice and counsel is necessary for the proper and effective functioning of your business. With this in mind, the relationship that your business has with its lawyers is an essential topic for discussion.

Although this is an important topic for your business, why are lawyers significant to CFOs? Should these relationships not be the responsibility of the business's General Counsel?

First, not all CFOs work in businesses that have a General Counsel (GC), and therefore the CFO is the key person who relates with outside legal counsel. Second, even in companies with a GC, the CFO may still be the key interlocutor with outside counsel for strategic or critically important issues. Third, in many companies that have internal legal counsel, the role is more of a compliance and contract review role than dealing with strategic or key issues.

Regardless of whether the CFO is the key person dealing with the company's lawyers or is involved only in issues that are strategic and critical to the finance team, a CFO needs to develop, nurture, and maintain legal counsel relationships for the benefit of the company.

Relationship Strategies

In 2011, I surveyed more than 30 CFOs about their relationships with outside counsel. Among the survey's results:

- Fifty percent of the CFOs had inside counsel.
- Sixty percent of surveyed CFOs were the main point of contact with outside counsel.

- Twenty-three percent of the CFOs who managed the relationship with outside counsel had internal legal counsel.
- Sixty-six percent of CFOs managed at least two or three relationships with outside counsel.

CFOs are influential participants in the relationship between a company and outside lawyers, and a number of CFOs manage the relationship for their company. With these relationships being important for the company, how should the CFO develop and nurture them?

Different lawyers have diverse specialties and bring specific value to the company based on their expertise, knowledge, experience, reputation, and cost. When CFOs choose to direct work to a lawyer, they need to select the best one for the company's specific needs. Generally, CFOs will preselect specific lawyers to direct work toward for different types of legal issues. For each lawyer the CFO chooses to work with, she needs to develop the relationship to the point where expectations for the delivery of work and the costs relating to the kind of work are understood up front.

It is also important that your outside legal counsel understand your business, in terms of both how you accomplish your goals as well as the challenges you continue to face. When your lawyer is working on your behalf, not being able to see the big picture can limit the value she can bring to the table. Also, you want your lawyer to look out for your best interests and provide you with information and connections that can have significant positive impact to the organization.

Impact of a Weak Relationship

Not using legal counsel when your company needs it can be an expensive proposition. When a company does not have strong relationships with its legal counsel, it may not get the level and timeliness of service it needs to deal with the issues properly. This can also be an expensive proposition.

When proper relationships are not established in advance of a company's needing legal assistance, the company suffers, as well. You may use the best lawyer in your city for a specific issue, but if he is not available when you need him, you do not have the best lawyer for your needs.

Impact of a Strong Relationship

If there is one thing that CFOs do not like about lawyers, it is their fees.

Sure, lawyers are interested in charging fees and making money on the work they do. But be aware that they are, in many cases, very social people and

List Your Key Legal Relationships: **Rate the Strength of Your Legal Relationships:**

1. _____   Very weak/Weak/Neither/Strong/Very strong
2. _____   Very weak/Weak/Neither/Strong/Very strong
3. _____   Very weak/Weak/Neither/Strong/Very strong

How much room for improvement do you have in your legal relationships?

A lot   _____
A little   _____
They are good, but could be   _____
better
They cannot be better   _____

Areas for improvement":

1. _____
2. _____
3. _____

Detail your plan for improving your legal relationships:

_____
_____
_____

enjoy building relationships and learning about the people they work with and the companies they work for. Investing this time with them will be very beneficial.

Once you have developed strong relationships with your lawyers, they will be more willing to charge more reasonable fees and invest in your business, because as you succeed, so will they.

OTHER OUTSIDE RELATIONSHIPS

The three relationships mentioned above are key outside relationships for the CFO, but they are certainly not the only ones. The following sections offer brief discussions on other relationships that deserve special mention.

Investment Banking

When companies grow to a certain size, they attract the attention of invest-ment bankers, who are interested in providing services such as assistance issuing securities or help with mergers and acquisitions. Relationships with investment bankers are very important when a company needs these or other specialized services they provide.

As CFO, you need to pay attention when investment bankers call, and use this as an opportunity to learn what they know about your business and your competitors. Even if you do not need the services these professionals provide now, you might need them one day. Having already built a relationship with these people allows you to call on them when you need them.

Tax Professionals

There are different types of taxes that companies have to pay. These can include taxes on income, sales, property, payroll, and imports. Not only are there different types of taxes, but different jurisdictions have their own rates and rules. When a company also operates outside of its country of origin, it faces new taxes with different rules that might even be written in different languages. To say that taxes are complicated can be an understatement.

Because this area can be so complex, it is not always possible for the finance team to stay on top of every tax and every issue. Guidance is needed to ensure that your company complies with the rules it faces in the locations it operates in. But compliance is not the only area in which companies may need help. Tax planning is important to minimize risks and maximize profits for the company in the regions where it operates.

It is important to build effective relationships with the professionals who advise you on your tax planning and help you comply with your filing requirements to ensure that you are paying taxes owed properly and on time. If you do not get the best out of the tax professionals advising you, you are leaving significant dollars on the table.

 CONCLUSION

- We discussed the importance of CFOs developing, nurturing, and main-taining relationships with people and organizations that provide important services to their businesses.

- We talked about the CFO's relationship with the company's auditor and discussed how to build a positive rapport with this person.
- We explained the value of building fruitful relationships with lenders and the impact they can have on your company.
- We reviewed the CFO's relationships with the company's lawyers, their importance to the company, and strategies on how to get the best from them.
- We listed items to review about your relationships with outsiders, and gave you a framework with which to plan for improvement.
- We gave examples of other relationships CFOs may have with outsiders, with the knowledge that different CFOs have different relationships on the outside that benefit the company.

CFOs need service providers outside of their business to help them and their company. Keeping an eye on these relationships is important as the CFO relies on them to support him in important ways. Spending time and effort to grow these relationships is a worthwhile investment for the CFO. Building trust with your outside providers can sometimes be a challenge, but when these people deliver for your business, you will know that the investment was certainly worth it.

Building and Developing Your Finance Team

T HE FOUNDATION OF SUPPORT for any Chief Financial Officer (CFO) is the finance team. A CFO cannot and should not go it alone. The finance team sits at the bottom of the relationship map (Chapter 8), not because it is the least important, but because it is the foundation of support for the CFO, making it possible for that key executive to deliver to the people he works for and works with.

My CFO advisors are in complete agreement with me regarding the importance of the finance team to the success of a CFO. Of all the questions that I asked them in preparation for this book, this is the only one where they all agree. One hundred percent of my CFO advisors believe that their finance teams are either important or very important for their success.

Here are some valuable comments made by my CFO advisors on the importance of the finance team to their success as CFO.

> If we're only as good as me, we're in trouble—and that's how I always approach my teams. By providing them with the means to achieve more and better results, the entire team improves its performance and both the team (and me) and the company benefit.

Without a strong team, you will not be able to satisfy the duties of a CFO; you will be too preoccupied getting transactional activities completed and will not be able to satisfy the needs of your boss or board.

My finance team is highly important to my success and the success of the organization as a whole. If I recruit, hire, and train the right team players to do their jobs, this will free up my time to focus on the business and strategic initiatives for the company. If you surround yourself with great team players, then you have access to more and better ideas in identifying problems and solutions. If I spend too much time in their areas doing their jobs, then I am detracting from the value of the finance function to the organization.

I can add value being strategic, etc., but the team must provide accurate information and make sure we are in compliance. Otherwise, I'm toast.

At this point, I hope you're convinced of how important a strong finance team is to the success of a CFO. If you're still not won over, reach out to me and let me know.

ELEMENTS OF A GREAT FINANCE TEAM

Knowing that your finance team is key to your success, what does a great finance team look like? Focusing on the following elements will provide the CFO with the ingredients she needs for a winning team.

People

It should be obvious that you need people to form a team. This is about having the right people, in the right place, at the right time.

Right People

There are many "*I*"s in *team*. If you've ever seen or been part of a dysfunctional team, you know firsthand that it is not just about having the right people. All of your "*I*"s need to work together to move from a collection of individuals to a team that functions well, preparing for the future while recording and reporting the past.

Right Place

In a world of cloud computing and virtual teams, the right place is not about location. Your people need to be in the right place in your company, allowing you to get the best value from them while they gain and grow personally and professionally.

You may have great people on your team who could contribute more value if they were working with other people or doing different work. Perhaps some of your people could benefit from working in another department and learning more about the business, and then coming back to finance where the long-term value of that knowledge and experience can accrue. Having an employee work in accounts receivable for 20 years may not be the most effective way of getting the best value over those 20 years.

Right Time

The right time is not from nine to five. It is about managing workflow and priorities, results and deliverables. As CFO, you must be on top of everything you were originally hired to be responsible for as well as every other project and company priority that has developed since then.

One of the great limiters on a CFO's potential is the lack of time to do everything that needs to get done. You need your soldiers to be available and ready to support you in your time of challenge and crisis so that you can make the tactical and strategic decisions necessary to achieve success.

Organized

The words *business* and *organization* are used interchangeably to describe the affairs of a company. While a business may be organized in a certain manner, is it well organized? Logically, the better organized a company is, the greater its probability of success.

Where a finance team has had the same structure over a long period of time, it cannot always take advantage of the strengths supporting it and the opportunities facing it. The organizational chart of a finance team should be written in pencil, not in stone. It is not about the boxes on the chart as much as it is about the people who are in the boxes. Which position reports to which is less important than which person works with whom.

A CFO does not gain value from a team that continues to be structured the way it was years ago when the people were different and the business was different. Your finance team needs to be organized in a manner that takes best advantage of the people currently on your team while focusing on delivering to the challenges that you face today and will face in the future.

Supported

What do finance people need to do their jobs? They need a place to work: an office to go to, a desk to work at, and a chair to sit on. There are also the tools with which to do their work: a telephone, a computer, and software programs. They also need to be supported.

The CFO Relationship Map puts the finance team at the bottom because the finance team supports the CFO. However, for the finance team to do its work, it needs to be supported by the CFO. In addition, each member of the team needs to be supported by his or her direct supervisors and leaders. For your finance team members to do their best job, they need to feel that you are supporting them so that they can support you.

What kind of support are we talking about? It's not about supporting them with office supplies. Really, it's about emotional support. Your team needs to *feel* that you care about them and will support them. Great CFOs are able to convey a giving image to all their staff while actually delivering on it. If the finance team feels that you are a slave driver, then its members will act as slaves and deliver value accordingly. When the CFO demonstrates her support of the team in her actions and words, the team members will be willing to give more of themselves to the company's success and the CFO's, as well.

Motivated

Think about the best work that you do. You're focused, dedicated, and committed to the task at hand. What motivates you to tackle that challenge and give it your all? You know very well what motivates you. What motivates the individuals on your team? That is hard to say, as it would depend on the person. How do you figure out what motivates a group of individuals? You can't. You can only guess.

However, there are basics of motivation that, when applied across a group of people, have the ability to have an impact. People want to be compensated fairly. They want to be appreciated for their efforts. Employees want to feel that their input is valued.

So, how do CFOs motivate their staffs? They should show their teams that they care about motivating them and are making a sincere effort to do so. I have seen too many finance professionals and executives who were thirsting for their CFO to show leadership and motivate them. Your people need you to push them in a good way to help you be a (more) successful CFO.

Results

You can have a great team with good people who are properly organized, supported, and motivated. In the end, if you don't get the results you need as CFO, it doesn't matter how wonderful your team is.

What results do you need? Sure, the company has to do well, but that is in the hands of the operators of your business. What does *results* mean to you? Think about what you want and need out of your finance team that will help you become the best CFO you can be. Really think about it, then let your team members know what you need from them. Make sure they know when they have been successful and celebrate the positive.

Your team wants to give you the results you need to be successful. Lead them to it.

THE COST OF A GREAT FINANCE TEAM

As keeper of the business's finances, the CFO needs to be prudent with financial resources. As CFO, you may be the person deputized with the power to say no to people inside and outside the firm. It may be easy to say no to others in the company, but CFOs need to be aware (and most are) that other executives will be scrutinizing their expenses if they're saying no to theirs.

The question really comes down to this: Can a CFO afford not to have an excellent finance function? To answer this question, I refer to research conducted by American Productivity and Quality Center (APQC), a nonprofit business benchmarking and research firm based in Houston, Texas. Its research shows that top-performing finance teams cost less to run than those that are mediocre or poorly functioning. Figure 12.1 graphically represents these results from the study.

CFOs have been pressured by their companies to do more with less. This research says that you can. While it may be counterintuitive to some, this research supports the idea that putting the effort into building an excellent finance function will end up costing you less.

As CFO, you hear "we need to spend money to make money" as the reason why people in your business are looking to maintain or increase their budgets and projects. Now, you have proof to show the people in your business that

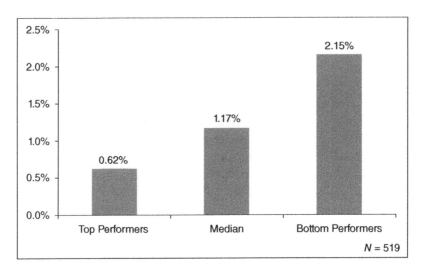

FIGURE 12.1 Total Cost of the Finance Function as a Percentage of Revenue

spending money now on a well-performing finance team that is efficient and effective will allow you to spend less money on your team in the future and deliver more value at the same time.

PLAN FOR A GREAT FINANCE TEAM

This APQC research does not mean that you will automatically save money if you spend money. It does mean that if you build a top-performing finance function, you will be able to benefit from the results—such as being able to afford top analytical talent—that a high level of process efficiency brings to you. You can only get to this performance nirvana if you plan for it.

Process and Technology

A great finance team needs the right people, surrounded by excellent processes, and supported by the appropriate technology to be successful. This should not be a surprise to anyone in Finance. But pulling together a great finance team doesn't happen by itself. We discussed elements of a great finance team built around people. However, just having great people will not make your finance team great, efficient, and effective. To be able to become a top-performing finance group that will give you the kind of cost advantage that will make you a star at your organization, you must have great processes and effective technology.

Processes and technology that make a difference do not happen by themselves. You must plan for them. Your plan for a great finance team must address these two critical components in addition to attracting great people. Great people can ensure that you have the processes and technology that can get you to CFO nirvana, but you need to give process and technology the importance they deserve and have a vision of what kind of end product your finance team will deliver.

Focus on the end product. Imagine for a moment what CFO nirvana looks like, with the ideal mix of people, process, and technology. Aim for this goal, share the idea, and help your people put a plan together to make it happen. The right mix will create a finance team that gives your company more for less. You can do it. Aim for it and you will achieve.

The Reality on the Ground

Do most CFOs have the best finance teams for their needs? I asked my CFO advisors if they have the best teams to support their needs. Most (56 percent) of my CFOs do not believe that they have the best finance team for their needs. I believe that this is representative of the reality on the ground. Take this situation and overlay it on the opportunity of how good you can look when you're efficient and effective (Figure 12.1), and the real world is not as pretty as it could be for many CFOs.

Here are some very interesting and valuable comments on the realities CFOs faced with their teams.

> As a small organization, we need to rely on only a few people and the level of expertise is not necessarily there. To improve that, a change in staffing would be required. This is difficult in a small organization as people's tasks are quite varied and tap into many areas of the business.
> Replace many junior, non-degreed staff with higher caliber people. I was able to replace an ineffective controller with a stellar person and these kinds of changes need to happen throughout the department—my controller and I spend way too much time on lower level work because we do not have the right staff in place. Being new to the organization, I see much change that is needed, but change is taking time.

The team was already in place when I started. They were developed in pre–private equity. They are hardworking but not accustomed to private equity requirements and more rigid reporting.

Yes, for now. But we are growing 100 percent year over year, so I have to keep thinking about growth and roles that will need to be added.

I am missing a couple of pieces. My right-hand person needs to be able to think out of the box and understand/change process as opposed to doing things by rote.

All CFOs face their own reality with their finance teams, but most would probably agree that their groups are not as effective as they could be.

Areas for Improvement

Most CFOs know they don't have the best team they can possibly have. Whether their finance team is close to being the best it can be or they need to put significant effort in to make it better, CFOs know there is always room for improvement.

For some real-life examples, I asked my CFO advisors: "If you could improve your finance team, what would you improve?" Here are some of their answers.

Their curiosity. Ask questions of the business, learn it, and understand it. The more knowledgeable they are, the more valuable they are to the business.

Stronger desire to learn and improve. Finance, particularly the accounting side, is a rather interesting breed compared to many of the functions I've managed. I tend to see a certain rigidity and, at times, resistance or even fear of change. Yet, embracing change is critical in as rapidly growing a company as we are.

Upgrade the staff I have too many long-term clerks who do not challenge the status quo or think of ways to improve. I need more eager, articulate professional accounting staff to take our organization to the next level.

Probably a rotation through the operations. I have a couple of direct reports who have done it and bring a wealth of knowledge and connections back to Finance and help increase our credibility.

Ability to navigate the gray areas. Everything is not black and white. As well as the ability to connect and be empathetic. Without these abilities, careers are limited.

I would improve our financial systems. However, if you are talking specifically about the team, I would improve their knowledge and interaction with the rest of the business/operations.

I would like to see more visibility across the function and more cross training. Sometimes, especially with lean teams, it is difficult to focus beyond the pressing day-to-day responsibilities.

Everyone has room to improve their finance team. What is the one thing that you need to improve on?

Define Your Needs

The first step in planning for a great finance team is understanding what you need from your finance team. As discussed in Chapter 7, a CFO needs a plan. When you know what you need to deliver on, you are in the right place to understand what your finance team needs to be able to deliver to support you in the delivery of your plan.

Writing this down is a critical component to help you succeed. As we said before, failing to plan is planning to fail. You need to define what you need in this process to ensure you get the support you need to make your plan happen.

Do you know what you need? Write it down. If you'd like me to review it for you, reach out to me. Having a plan is a critical component for your success. Your success is my success. I'd be happy to invest my time.

Zero-Based Team Building

Zero-based budgeting (ZBB) is a tool used by companies to develop a budget by not simply redoing last year's budget. ZBB helps you build a budget that throws out the baby with the bathwater. This fresh start helps spur your imagination and build the budget for your enterprise in the best way possible.

Finance people know about ZBB, even if they have never implemented it themselves. You can use the same concept for building your team. Think of this as zero-based team building.

You know your needs, because you have written them down. Now you can, on paper at least, build your dream team. Imagine for a moment that you had no impediments to creating your finance dream team. What should your organization chart look like? What kind of people would be the leaders of your team? Think about it. Dream. Wouldn't this team be a great help in delivering on your plan?

Understand Your Current Team

In planning for a great finance team, you need to understand what you currently have. While your ideal finance team can be created in your mind and on paper using zero-based team building, the reality is that you have an existing team, with its strengths and weaknesses. This is your real starting point.

What are the strengths and weaknesses of your team? To understand this, you need to know what your team as a whole is able to deliver to you and the entire business. Think about what your team accomplishes and does well.

While your finance team should be a sum greater than its parts, the parts are important, too. Identify the key people in your group, and understand what they do really well. If the sum is really greater than its parts, you will have a team that has strengths together that cannot be accounted for by the individual leaders on your team.

You can make this assessment in your head; however, writing it down and organizing it will be beneficial to visualizing the value of the human assets you have to work with.

Identify Gaps

You have created, on paper, what you think your dream team should look like. You have also made an assessment of the strengths of your team as a whole as well as the strengths of your finance leaders.

When you compare your ideal team to what you currently have, you will notice the gaps. Clearly identify and create a list of the gaps. You now know what you have to tackle to build a great finance team. Put these gaps in order of priority or urgency. You now have a list of areas you need to tackle to build that great finance team you need to support your quest to become a successful CFO.

The Realistic Team

These gaps could be significant. At this point in the exercise, you may feel that the gaps are too great between where you are with your team and where you want to be. You should not despair. Just because you don't have the ideal team, it doesn't mean that you cannot build it over time. The words "over time" are important to keep in mind as you plan for a great finance team. You cannot accomplish your goals for a great finance team all at once. You need to truly understand where you want to go, and then identify the steps needed to get you there.

In the interim, between the current and ideal state for your finance team, you need to be realistic. You can only do what you can do with the assets you currently have in place. With the end in sight, you need to take a look at your current team and see how you can get the best from it. There may be changes you can make quickly with little pain based on the strengths of your current team.

It is possible that you can identify ways to shift responsibilities around and rearrange the deck chairs to improve your team's functioning in the interim. Just keep in mind that the chess game you are playing has to have as its end goal where you want to be. You don't want to be in a situation where you are going to make a change that will negatively impact where you want to go. These changes cannot be made lightly, but when proper thought is put into them, you can improve the results achieved by your current team members.

Plan for Growth

At this point, you have identified the most realistic finance group you can organize to be able to add value today. You've envisioned the ideal state for your team with your vision for a zero-based team. Before discussing what you need to do to be able to get to that ideal team, you need to keep in mind that your ideal state should not be set in stone.

Your vision for the best possible team to support you and the business is only ideal at the time you created it in your head and put it on paper. You need to be open to changes in your business and the demands on your finance group. Your business may shed a division or open a new geographic territory. Key staff can leave your team. These and other events can put you in a situation where your plan may have to be seriously reconsidered.

Your plan is only current at the moment you create it. Your ideal team can be a moving target. Keeping this in mind will allow you to refresh your strategy for building the best team as you continue to move, change, and grow.

 BUILDING YOUR FINANCE TEAM

You have done your homework and you know what your ideal team looks like. You know the gaps you face in moving your team along the path from where it is to where you want it to be.

Think about the finance team you want to build as a complicated puzzle. There are three ways to build your ideal finance team. Each of these approaches is necessary, although, depending your current situation and where you want to go, you may be focusing on one of these elements more than the others.

Hire

When you are missing key pieces in your puzzle, you may have no choice but to find a way to acquire the missing pieces. Hiring is one component of a strategy that will help you build your team.

You may think that because my profession is executive search, I am a big proponent of hiring. This is true only to the extent that you do not have access to the talent internally to be able to take your team to where you need it to be. Hiring is not always the best solution to building your team.

The biggest challenge with hiring is that it is easy to hire, but hard to hire right. We have all seen situations where investments in hiring were made that did not work out. The reasons for unsuccessful hiring can be many. A complete explanation of these reasons would be beyond the scope of this chapter and book. However, from my perspective, most hiring failures happen for two reasons.

One reason for a failed hire is that the understanding of the real need was flawed from the beginning. When managers hire and make a successful match for the wrong need, it should not be a surprise that the person hired cannot and will not deliver what the finance team really needs. I have been witness to one too many situations where senior finance professionals hire poorly. When they do not take the time to map out where they want to take their team and do not understand their real needs, they are setting themselves up for a failed hire.

Another reason for a botched hire is when a hiring manager understands the needs correctly but hires the wrong person to deliver. When the person hired does not have the skills to match the needs of the role and the company, it is an indicator that the person or people responsible for the hiring did not properly assess what the new employee would be able to accomplish. While you, the reader, may not have been guilty of this, many finance professionals hire based on gut, not a clear-headed assessment of the candidate being considered.

Things that can influence the instinct-based hiring decisions of a senior finance professional include, but are not limited to:

- Previous relationship with the candidate
- The work and/or educational experience of the candidate, with a bias to hire people who have a similar background to the leader doing the hiring

Hiring well is not easy, but it is critical if you are to build the right team for your needs. I highly recommend that CFOs build relationships with internal or external resources that can add value to the hiring process and improve your chances for hiring success. Your human resources team can provide you with the support you need to acquire the important puzzle pieces you are missing. If your HR team is not able to give you what you need, I recommend working with an external search firm that understands you, your business, and the role you are hiring for, and has the relevant delivery experience to add significant value in the process.

Retain

The best way not to have to hire new employees is to make sure that you retain those you want to keep. Managers may want their employees to stay as long as they want them, but employers do not control whether or when their employees want to leave. If you are a finance executive, you have undoubtedly experienced a situation where a valued employee has left your firm. In many cases when this happens, you can be left in the lurch. Nod your head up and down if you have faced this situation personally. I thought so.

As CFO, it is not possible to guarantee that the employees you want and need to remain with your firm will do so. However, as CFO, you do have an ability to impact your rate of retention.

SUPERSTARS

When it comes to retention, you want to keep your best and most valuable employees. You do not, however, want to keep *all* your employees. Identifying your superstars, acknowledging them, and investing in their continued development gives you an opportunity to keep your best staff members and make them even better. This effort may take a lot of work on your part as well as time and expense. This is not about whether you can afford to. It's about whether you can afford not to.

Expectations

You may remember that in Chapter 8, we discussed the elements of relationship management. You know from the discussion in that chapter about the CFO Relationship Map, and you also know that your finance team is the supporting foundation for your role as CFO. Managing expectations is a critical element for successful relationship management and is especially important for the people who support you.

You cannot get your team to deliver what you expect of them if you don't clearly communicate what you need them to deliver for you. When employees are not clear on what you want from them, not only will they not be able to deliver, they will be frustrated that they are not being given the opportunity to do so.

Motivation

Motivation is a personal choice. I cannot motivate you to follow the path and strategies that I have set out in this book. You have to *want* to be motivated by what I have shared with you for my book to have an impact on you and your career. My goal is to inspire you, show you that it is easier than you might think to accomplish these goals, tell you that I believe in you (which I do), and give you examples that show you that if others can achieve success, you can, too. All you need to do is listen to what I have to say. Whether you take my words to heart and change your approach to your success as a senior finance executive is up to you.

You have a similar role to play with your employees. In many, if not most cases, you, once upon a time, were in their shoes. You did their work. You worked for a really great CFO, just like they do. It is your responsibility to inspire, guide, believe in, and mentor your team.

You may never know if your team members stayed because of you. If you don't make the effort to motivate them, you will surely fail. Make the effort.

Three *R*s: Responsibility, Recognition, and Respect

Control freaks are not successful in the long term. Successful leaders give their people responsibility and hold them accountable. Strong managers recognize outstanding effort, even in the face of failure. Respected leaders gain respect by giving respect first. These three *R*s need to be the rules by which successful CFOs run their teams. You cannot be a successful CFO if you do not live by these rules.

Compensation

Effective and fair compensation practices allow you to not only hire the best people, but keep them, as well. Career satisfaction is not driven by compensation alone, but it does have a big impact on overall job contentment. Paying well may not be a guarantee that you will keep the people you want to keep, but paying poorly will certainly reduce your ability to keep the best.

Corporate finance professionals are fortunate because their skills are very transferrable and not dependent on the industry they work in. Other careers may not have the same advantage. The opportunities for a biochemical engineer are generally more limited than the opportunities available to the people who work for you.

Cull the Herd

If you want to keep the best, don't keep the worst. The people on your team know the individuals who are coasting or worse. On your path to creating a high-performing finance team, you do not gain anything by keeping the underperformers. Culling the herd will motivate your superstars.

People Leave Managers

It is rare that people leave companies. People leave managers. If you're not such a great manager, or the leaders on your team who manage in your name are not as good as you need them to be, there is a good chance that your retention rate is lower than it should be.

Grow

Growing your own finance team is more like growing a garden than planting crops. I do not have a green thumb, but I can appreciate the tender love, care, effort, and thought that gardeners put into their gardens. Watering, fertilizing, weeding, and pruning are all necessary parts of growing a garden. Certain plants do well next to some plants but not others. Some need different conditions. Some thrive in different climates or seasons. A great CFO under-stands that all of these concepts apply to growing a great finance team.

Developing your finance team is the key to getting them to grow. There are different methods through which you can develop your team, and we discuss the details of developing your finance group next.

 DEVELOP YOUR TEAM

Developing your team is not simple. It takes a sustained effort over a period of time, using different tools and strategies to develop both the individuals on your team and your team as a whole. As CFO this is something you need to seriously invest in.

We discussed previously that you want and need to keep your superstars, and to do so you need to invest in their growth. Do CFOs provide their superstars with what they need to shine and grow? I asked my CFO advisors this very question, and thankfully 83 percent of them say that they do. Here are some of their comments on the topic.

> In our current organization, we do not have any superstars. We have tried to empower the middle management layer to allow them to succeed and shine, but this has not happened.
>
> The problem I see is people have become comfortable in their positions and when you push them to grow or take on new tasks they are afraid of failure. I explain that I will be working with them and overseeing the task, and if it fails, it is my fault. People are afraid to step outside their comfort zones.
>
> I'm working on it. For example, I saw that someone in accounting, with an accounting background, was growing stale in that function. However, she also had a real sense of the business and asked the most strategic questions. Meanwhile, FP&A had no one with real accounting skills (and skill with our systems) on the team, so I transferred her over and have been supporting her growth there. She's loving it and shining.
>
> My highest-potential people (controller, finance director) either are not aggressive in growing their own careers or are too reluctant and cautious to step up, hire up, and grow to capacity.
>
> A development/career plan is important to retaining and developing your A-team players. If you don't have a plan, then you risk losing those players to other organizations that are looking for high performers.
>
> While accepting that some superstars will leave to further their careers, I never want them to leave because of a lack of opportunity or investment. I believe in continuous performance management to avoid surprises and proactively manage careers.
>
> We develop folks by throwing them into the deep end and seeing if they can make it to shore. When they do, we reward them greatly and provide significant new challenges.
>
> We have very few superstars. I am working to develop the people with the most potential, but no real shining stars to speak of—

> my task right now is to get the staff to at least reach their
> potential.

As our finance team is lean, this leaves little time for development
other than learning on the job.

I emphasize education and networking opportunities as well as
crossfunctional training to put aggressive career paths in front
of our stars.

I provided these examples to show you that CFOs like you face different challenges and limitations when it comes to developing their finance teams. However, all of these CFOs understand their current situations, both in terms of the talent of their people and the resources available to develop that talent.

Current Gaps

Earlier in this chapter we discussed how to plan for a great finance team. In that section, we mentioned that it is important to identify what gaps exist on your finance team between its current state and its ideal state (zero-based team building).

When it comes to the development of the individuals on your team, a similar analysis needs to be made. The *gap analysis* that needs to be made is: what the potential is of the people you've identified as worth developing, and what they need to get from where they are today to where they can go.

Growth Goals

The gaps in skills of individuals you want to develop point to the areas for further development. However, not all gaps need to be bridged, and not all bridges need to be built at once.

As finance leader, you need to identify what you feel are the most appropriate goals for your employees to focus on and support their further development. These growth goals should be chosen in cooperation with your employees. As the people who will benefit from this effort, they will need to buy into it to ensure their personal success.

For the development of your people to meet your goals, you need to know what benefits you want and need from their continued development. Your team development priorities should have a strong correlation to the development areas for your people. Because your people make up your team, the gaps that you need filled should be a key component in driving the investment in developing your staff. Before having a discussion with your key employees about what they need to do for their own success, know what you need from them so that both your employees and your team as a whole are successful.

Development efforts need to be looked at from a short-, medium-, and long-term perspective. As CFO, however, you should be more concerned with the short- and medium-term objectives.

METHODS TO DEVELOP YOUR TEAM

Knowing what your people need to further develop is a great start. You have different options to develop your team and the people on it. Each method for development works better in some instances and for some individuals. When choosing the methods for development, you will need to assess which of them are suited to deliver the best outcome for a specific employee and the team. Working with only one of these development methods will limit your ability to achieve the best results.

Formal Training

We are fortunate to be living in a world where we have many options for formalized training. In the past, this type of training could only be done in a classroom setting, where the limitations of time and location would make it difficult for the finance team to take advantage of it. Today, in addition to traditional classroom training, technology enables remote and on-demand learning and provides many more options that are reasonably priced.

Identifying whether there are training tools for the area of development you want to invest in is a Google search away. Knowing whether this type of development investment will actually make the gap shrink or disappear is a harder question to answer up front.

These tools can be more helpful for skill shortcomings that are not company specific. Formal training in taxation is a good example of knowledge that can be acquired from the outside that can make a difference to your firm. In areas that need to be developed that are particular to your company, an outside training course may not be sufficient or effective.

Some companies offer their own finance leadership training that provides formalized training for the finance team. The most well-known of these programs is the one at General Electric. You can read more about GE's Financial Leadership Program in *CFO* magazine's article, "Oiling the Leadership

Machine at GE" (http://ww2.cfo.com/training/2011/12/oiling-the-leadership-machine-at-ge). GE is a great company. Unless your company is of the size and scope of GE, your budget for developing your finance leaders may not allow you to put together such a comprehensive effort. However, your company may be of the size that you should consider developing some sort of formalized training for your finance team. Think about it. The benefits might significantly outweigh the costs. A formalized training program can help you attract high-potential recruits to your team, as well as help retain your upcoming leaders.

On-the-Job Training

This type of development is very popular within finance groups. The effectiveness of this kind of training, however, varies greatly. One method for training on the job can include showing employees what they need to know and then monitoring and reviewing their progress along the way to ensure they are learning properly and effectively. Another method is for the senior person to give the junior person the challenge of accomplishing a particular goal with little guidance and a lot of motivation, which can be similar to teaching someone to swim by pushing the individual into the deep end. Both of these methods can be considered extreme, and they can both be effective depending on what needs to be taught and the capabilities of the student.

The biggest challenge with this type of training happens when there is no structure for it. As we have seen many times in this book, failing to plan is planning to fail. The method of on-the-job training is less important than having objectives that are well-communicated and clear. On-the-job training can only be successful when you can measure success against predetermined goals.

Mentorship

Ask successful CFOs if they have had mentors during their careers and they will not only say yes, they will remember their mentors well going back decades. Your future leaders need mentorship to grow and mature as corporate finance professionals. Where formalized and on-the-job training impact hard skills, mentorship deals with the important learning needed for the development of soft skills.

We all need guidance. Future leaders in your finance group need to find people that they can approach to work out the finer details of relationship management and firm politics. Those who have been successful in your organization and others can provide valuable information, resources, and feedback that can help your up-and-comers become better professionals.

Coaching

Sometimes mentorship is not enough. The higher up a finance professional moves within an organization, the fewer people are available to mentor him. Even if mentors are available, a controller reporting to a vice president may not be able to get objective advice or guidance from her direct boss.

In Chapter 7 we discussed executive coaching for the CFO. Many of the value points mentioned for CFO coaching apply to your superstars. I have been approached by CFOs to coach their future senior finance leaders. These CFOs know how difficult it is to be CFO and to become CFO, and appreciate the value that a professional executive coach brings to someone who has the potential to become a Chief Financial Officer in the future.

 CFO SUCCESSION

If you are a CFO, one day in the future you will leave your current role. You may move up in the company. You may move out. When that happens, do you know who will take over as CFO?

If you're reading this and you're not a CFO, you may be asking, "Why should CFOs care who takes their place when they are no longer at the company?" CFOs are very caring and responsible people. They feel a personal responsibility to the company, its shareholders, employees, and anyone else whose livelihood depends on the success of the company they work for. CFOs take this responsibility seriously and very personally.

The most effective option for a company hiring its next CFO is to promote someone internally *if* that individual is the best person for the job. CFOs have a responsibility to their employers to ensure that they can be replaced if needed. The CFO chair is too important to any company to be left empty.

The two possible ways for a company to hire its next CFO are to hire an existing Chief Financial Officer, or you can grow your own. If you properly plan for a great finance team, this should include developing and planning for your heir.

Do you know who could succeed you when you move on from your CFO role? Almost 60 percent of my CFO advisors know who would succeed them, while 92 percent of CFOs can identify their superstars. My takeaway from these two statistics is that over 30 percent of CFOs have superstars that they have not put on the path to becoming CFOs. This should remind CFOs that they not only need to develop their superstars to do the job today but need to provide them with resources that help them grow into a role where they can replace the CFO.

The preferred model for CFO succession allows you to identify and develop your heir as well as a spare. Depending on person X to be the future finance leader in your business is like putting all your eggs in one basket. Ideally, you need to develop more than one person. You should work to give your company a choice when the time comes to replace you, not present it with a *fait accompli*, as this will likely backfire.

We discussed methods for the development of your finance team previously, but you may want to single out your superstars for special treatment. Creating a high-energy, valuable, and focused development program that will prepare your superstars for successful careers as CFOs will only benefit your company and will certainly be a key retention driver for these heavyweights. Investing in these super-people does not guarantee that they will stay, but not making the investment will guarantee that they will take a better opportunity if it finds them.

Executive coaching is an excellent way to provide a valuable benefit to finance superstars, and 75 percent of my CFO advisors who have superstars agree. CFOs may feel that they are the best person to coach them, yet there is value in having someone from the outside coach these up-and-comers.

Finance superstars need to focus on developing their soft skills as well as really learning the business. CFOs should not be hired, in almost all cases, because of their technical skills but because of their ability to get things done. Learning the business provides your company's potential next CFO with the ability to truly understand how the role of finance can add value to the company. CFOs, as we discussed in Chapter 1, need to be strategists, leaders, and advisors. If your up-and-coming finance talent learn how to become strategists, leaders, and advisors, they are better equipped to be a CFO in the near future.

HOW DO I BECOME A CFO?

This book provides CFOs with guidance on how to become a better and more successful Chief Financial Officer. The audience for this book is also those who would like to become CFO in the future. I would like to address the future CFO before we conclude this guide.

You have already taken an important first step to becoming CFO—you read this book. If I have accomplished what I have set out to do, you now have a much better insight into the mind of the CFO and the challenges these professionals face on a daily basis. Compared to your peers who hope to become CFO but have not read this book, you have a distinct competitive advantage.

An important factor in becoming a CFO is to understand what a CFO does. I mentioned in Chapter 1 that different companies need different CFOs to meet their needs. In the company you currently work for, try, to the extent possible, to understand what your CFO does. You may not be privy to everything, but be aware. You can learn something about what this individual does by seeing your CFO in action, or by seeing the end results of your CFO's work, and trying to figure out what the steps could have been on the road to his accomplishments. If you want to become a CFO, learn the CFO game.

Outside of your current employer, identify CFOs whom you want to emulate. The financial press and the Internet provide a lot of interesting information on CFOs and their career moves, as well as the strategic choices made by a company and the results of those choices. Some corporate finance professionals tell me that they follow my weekly *CFO Moves* blog to get an appreciation of the CFO market and how they get hired and move along in their careers. If you want to become a CFO, emulate other CFOs.

You have read earlier in this chapter a discussion on development of the finance team. What are the skills you will need to become CFO? What does your current skill set look like? What are you missing to bridge your own skills gap? Building your own CFO skills is important if you want to become a CFO. You can ask your employer for help in building these skills, but ultimately, you are responsible for your career. If you want to become a CFO, learn CFO skills.

During football season in the United States, Sunday is a day for armchair quarterbacks. You can be an armchair CFO every day in your office. Understand the moves, be aware of the plays, think the strategy through, know the players, and respect the competition. If you want to become CFO, act as if you were the CFO.

 ## YOUR FIRST CFO ROLE

On the road to becoming CFO, the biggest challenge finance people face is getting hired for their first CFO role. If you never have your first opportunity as CFO, it is harder to be considered as CFO material for opportunities in the future. In my weekly *CFO Moves* blog, I see different ways through which finance professionals are becoming first-time Chief Financial Officers.

Finance leaders can get promoted internally upon the current CFO leaving, either as the permanent replacement or on an interim basis. While there is no permanency in any job, you would prefer becoming CFO on a permanent basis as opposed to an interim one. Although interim CFOs have greater opportunity to become CFOs in the future, the chance for them to become permanent CFOs at their current employers is not guaranteed. New CFOs who are promoted are given an interim CFO title when the company does not have the confidence that this person is the right one for the senior finance chair. The options that exist for a finance leader who is promoted to interim CFO are being hired as permanent CFO, returning to his previous position, or leaving the company, whether his choice or the company's. Being interim CFO can be a stepping-stone to becoming a full-time Chief Financial Officer, even if it ends up being for another company.

First-time CFO roles can be had for those with senior-level finance experience who come from larger companies and are hired by smaller companies. This kind of move can give you the opportunity to become a bigger fish in a smaller pond. Once you have proven yourself as a big fish, a larger pond may be interested in inviting you to swim in its waters.

In larger companies, the business unit CFO is a good opportunity to prove yourself as a CFO. Your business unit may be a small piece of the company, but by itself, may be larger than many other companies in your industry. Becoming business unit CFO allows you to act as a real CFO with some minor differences from a corporate-level CFO.

However you get your first CFO position, chances are that it won't be your last. Focus on becoming and maintaining yourself as a successful CFO.

CONCLUSION

- We reconfirmed the importance of a strong finance team to the success of a CFO.
- We identified the elements of a great finance team.
- We discussed the costs of a great finance team and learned that high-performance teams cost relatively less to run with more value to the business.
- We learned how to plan for a great finance team, as well as what needs to be done to build one.
- We talked about the role of superstars on the finance team and how to retain and develop them further.
- We mentioned methods for training and developing within a finance team.
- We reviewed the importance of preparing for an eventual CFO succession.

▪ We gave additional tips to future CFOs on what they need to do to prepare themselves for eventually becoming CFO.

CFOs can only be successful with strong finance teams that support their objectives. Envisioning the ideal team and understanding the value of the current players on your team allows you to prepare a development plan to improve your current staff and attract others. Hiring and retention are key areas that CFOs need to concern themselves with to ensure their teams will support them today and in the future. The finance team can sometimes be overlooked by a CFO aiming for success. Getting the best out of your team requires an investment in your team members. If they succeed, so will you.

Not only does this conclusion end a chapter, it ends this book, as well. We have touched on many subjects that are important to your success as CFO. You can use this guide as a reference when looking for direction and inspiration, or as the impetus for a holistic approach to renewing your commitment to your success as CFO. I wrote this book with the goal of making a difference in the careers of CFOs. If this book helped you, I am grateful for the opportunity to do so. Thank you, and I'm looking forward to following your CFO success.

Bibliography

Bradt, George B.; Check, James A.; Pedraza, Jorge E. *The New Leader's 100-Day Action Plan: How to Take Charge, Build Your Team, and Get Immediate Results.* Hoboken, Hoboken, NJ: John Wiley & Sons, 2011.

Huffman, Kent. *8 Mandates for Social Media Marketing Success.* Austin, TX: C-Suite Press, 2012.

Joel, Mitch. *Six Pixels of Separation: Everyone Is Connected. Connect Your Business to Everyone.* New York: Hachette Book Group, 2009.

Lindsay, Hugh. *Financial Aspects of Governance: What Boards Should Expect from CFOs.* Toronto, Canada: Canadian Institute of Chartered Accountants, 2004. (http://www.cica.ca/focus-on-practice-areas/governance-strategy-and-risk/cfo-series/item12316.pdf)

McCann, David. "Oiling the Leadership Machine at GE." *CFO Magazine*, December 16, 2011. (http://ww2.cfo.com/training/2011/12/oiling-the-leadership-machine-at-ge/)

McCafferty, Joseph. "Finance vs. Marketing." *CFO Magazine*, May 1, 2007. (http://www.cfo.com/article.cfm/9059269)

Rath, Tom; Conchie, Barry. *Strengths-Based Leadership: Great Leaders, Teams, and Why People Follow.* New York: Gallup Press, 2008.

"The True Measure of Finance Function Excellence: Deliver Value Efficiently." Houston, Texas. American Productivity and Quality Center (APQC), 2012. (http://www.apqc.org/knowledge-base/documents/true-measure-finance-function-excellence-deliver-value-efficiently)

Wensley, Karen. *The Power of Personal Branding for Career Success.* Toronto, Canada: Canadian Institute of Chartered Accountants, 2012.

About the Author

Samuel Dergel is an executive search consultant and executive coach who focuses on the office of the Chief Financial Officer (CFO). He works with Stanton Chase International, an executive search firm serving companies worldwide from more than 70 offices. Dergel started his career with Ernst & Young and went on to financial leadership roles in the manufacturing and technology sectors before joining the world of executive search in 2002. He joined Stanton Chase in 2012.

Dergel is an active Certified Public Accountant (Maine, since 1996), active Chartered Professional Accountant and Chartered Accountant (Quebec, since 1995), and a Certified Personnel Consultant (since 2010). He received his Graduate Diploma in Public Accountancy in 1994 and his Bachelor of Commerce with a major in Accounting and a minor in Finance in 1992, both from McGill University in Montreal, Canada.

Dergel is an active blogger and social media leader on the topic of the Chief Financial Officer. He has been sought out by the media and as a speaker for his knowledge and insights. His expertise in understanding the challenges that CFOs face and the needs of companies hiring them allows him to assist his clients with hiring the most appropriate Chief Financial Officer and other senior financial executives.

Dergel publishes two blogs focused on the CFO. If you like what he has to say in this book, you will appreciate his CFO blog (http://blog.dergelcfo.com), which provides an insider's insight into the mind of the CFO. Dergel also publishes the very popular *CFO Moves* (http://cfomoves.com), a comprehensive weekly report that tracks CFO movement across the United States.

To learn more about Dergel or to contact him directly, you can reach him on LinkedIn. You can also follow him on Twitter: @DergelCFO.

Index

Printed and bound by CPI Group (UK) Ltd, Croydon, CR0 4YY

16/04/2025

14658508-0002